Also by Brian Peterson

move over, girl

Said to be "a must read for every college student,"
Move Over, Girl shows the revealing thoughts and
hilarious antics of Tony Norris, a campus player caught up
in more than his fair share of "extracurricular activities."

spoken words

Troi is the poet-teacher activist. Jay is the aspiring
novelist. Nichelle is the no-nonsense fly girl. Stephon
is the corporate player. The neo-classic allure of
Love Jones meets the heyday of MTV's *The Real World*
in this insightful urban story about sharing space
and sharing souls.

THE AFRICAN AMERICAN STUDENT'S GUIDE TO EXCELLENCE IN COLLEGE

BRIAN PETERSON

chance 22

ISBN 0-9664587-2-9

Third Printing.

Learn, then teach.

So…you're probably sitting there thinking, "Why should I read this book? I know what I'm doing." Guess what? You've got a lot to learn.

Investing a few hours to read this book is going to save you a lot of time and frustration in the long run.

Don't push this book to the side. No matter if you're a freshman just starting out, or heading into your senior year, read this book <u>now</u> so you can make the most out of your college experience.

INTRODUCTION

- Thinking about continuing your education after high school, but nervous about what lies ahead?
- You're in! You made it to college! Now what?
- Freshman year didn't go quite as expected? What can you do to turn it around?
- Heading into your junior year – how do you make the most of your last two years?
- Okay, now you're a senior. Did you miss anything? And what can you expect from life after college?
- Oh no. Looks like you might not make it out of here in four years after all. What should you do?

Welcome to *The African American Student's Guide to Excellence in College*. I've been there, so I know what you're going through (or will be going through soon). What not only got me to the finish line, but helped me to excel academically and socially, was a determination to succeed, sound study strategies, utilizing my resources, and knowing who I was and what I wanted. It might seem like a simple formula, but trust me, it takes a while to figure out all of the pieces, especially when you're "learning on the job." Plus, when you have to deal with a dozen things at once, as is often the case in college, it can become extremely difficult, even overwhelming at times, trying to get it together. That's why I wrote this book, to help make the road to graduation a little bit easier.

Did you know that **after 6 years of college, only 46% of African American students earn their degrees**?[1] Only 17% of all African American adults have a college degree.[2] Meanwhile, African Americans make up 40.1% of all inmates in Federal prisons.[3]

It's alarming how many stories I've personally heard about African American students who didn't graduate due to poor grades, financial struggles, personal hardships, or other circumstances. Others take time off (either voluntarily or due to academic probation), or labor through five or more years of school, often due to a lack of focus, advising, and support. Further, there is another set of Black students who graduate on time, but do not feel that their college experience was as fulfilling or beneficial as it should have been. This is more frequently found at larger, predominantly white institutions, where African American students may constantly feel like they're outsiders looking in.

What's worse is the silence on these issues. We assume once Jamal from down the block has gone off to school, everything is going to be wonderful, and that he's well on his way to making it. The reality is that Jamal is more likely to return home without his degree than with it. Nearly seven out of ten African American males who enter college do not graduate![4]

Why are the numbers so low?

There are several explanations for the low retention and graduation rates of African American students. From the student's perspective, paying for college and feeling comfortable (academically confident, socially adjusted) are the top two issues. If a student, African American or otherwise, comes from an under-resourced high school, or one that didn't emphasize college prep, they may be bright and academically capable, but not as academically equipped, nor even know what to expect from college. Additionally, for Black students attending predominantly white institutions, not only is there the issue of figuring out the books, but also feelings of racial isolation, neglect by professors and departments, and cultural shock.

Colleges and universities that address these concerns by providing mentoring, student/faculty interactions, academic support, social outlets, and promoting cultural acceptance tend to have higher retention rates.[5] These institutions recognize that students must not be "cut loose" and left on their own when entering college. Consistent support structures must be in place to nurture students throughout the course of their collegiate experience. Additionally, at the outset of school, students must clearly understand what they're getting into, and what is expected of them. Many students do not. This book seeks to change that, and reading it is an important first step that every African American college student should take.

The goal of this book (and how to use it)

My concept is straightforward. I want to show students how to maximize their study efforts so they can earn the best grades possible, efficiently use their time, and take greater advantage of the social, cultural, and networking opportunities available while in college. Typically, instead of outlining one specific method or way of doing things, I've suggested effective strategies that students can incorporate into their lives and make their own. I've also broken down the common mistakes that many students make. We don't all do things the same way, and at the end of the day, we all must make our own choices. My intent is to provide a framework that will help students make informed decisions and achieve the best results. By focusing on excellence, it's my belief that not only will more students remain in school, but they will also reach their full potential, graduate with better grades and have a more well-rounded and positive overall experience.

Whether you're a senior at San Diego State, a junior at Yale, a sophomore at Spelman, or a freshman going part-time to Community College, there's something inside this book that will help you to take control of your future. Additionally, there's information specific to students' special interests and activities (notes for athletes, student leaders) and also a chapter for school administrators, faculty, and parents.

High school students interested in taking a look at what college life is all about should also sit down with a copy of this book. Read it today, then re-read it at the beginning of each semester to get refocused. Also, at any point during the course of a semester, look up a particular topic that you may need assistance with, such as time management, or reading comprehension. As you'll learn in these pages, studying, and being able to apply what you've learned, is a *process*, not a one-time event.

ONE. WHY THIS BOOK?

There are a few ways to look at this question. First, *why write a study guide for college students?* These kids got into college, and are America's "best and brightest," right? Shouldn't they be able to figure it out on their own?

This is far from true, as pointed out in the introduction. College is a world away from high school, but most students don't fully understand that until they get to college and see it firsthand. In high school, I remember waiting until the night before a test to start studying, then getting a good score. That's not going to get it done in college.

Studying in college is a systematic process that involves attending lectures (and sometimes additional recitations or labs), going to office hours, studying on your own throughout the semester, forming study groups, and using academic resources on campus like tutoring and extra help sessions. Unfortunately, it takes many students a few poor exam grades to figure this out. For others, collegiate activities like parties and student organizations may become distractions instead of extracurricular fun. Combine that with the fact that mommy and daddy aren't in your face to keep you in check, and you could end up spending the last two years of college trying to make up for wasting the first two.

It doesn't have to be like that. If you know what you're getting into, you can design a personal plan for success. But how are you supposed to know the deal about college if you've never been before? It's quite unfair to expect an incoming freshman to know what's going on. It's even difficult for juniors and seniors to keep it all together with the fast-paced, pressure-filled environment, especially when they have no one in their corner providing guidance. Semesters begin and end in the blink of an eye. If you don't take the time to set goals, map out a plan, and evaluate your progress, it will be over before you know it, and you'll be looking at another grade sheet of the same old thing.

This book will help you to take control of the outcome, and get the grades that you are capable of earning.

So, *why write a guide specifically for African American college students?* Do we study differently than students of other races? The short answer is "not necessarily." Solid academic techniques such as attending class regularly, paying attention, using your available help resources and knowing how to properly prepare for an exam are applicable across the racial board. There is, however, significant research on learning styles which suggests that certain approaches to learning may be more effective with African American students. We will talk about these later.

For now, it's important to understand that this book is not simply about study practices. Success in college requires a **holistic** focus. Your social well-being, your family life, your finances, your health, your activities, and your frame of mind all play major roles in your academic career.

With that said, there are experiences unique to African Americans, before entering college and after, that make this book necessary. For example, an African American student at a predominantly white institution may feel an increased pressure to participate in numerous student activities and organizations for the simple fact that there's a much smaller pool of Black students to work with. Also, there's the constant burden of being stereotyped or singled-out, which can have a tremendous effect on your interactions and your ability to feel "at home" while at school. And finally, in my opinion, Black families tend to view higher education, and education in general, more compassionately, due to our historical denial of access to educational opportunities. For example, you may be one of a few, or perhaps even *the first* one to go to college in your family. This landmark achievement will generate a tremendous amount of pride and emotion, but may also create additional pressure since you are already dealing with leaving home for the first time, probably unsure of exactly what lies ahead. These are just a small sample of stories. We'll discuss these, and more, in later chapters.

Next up, why *this* book – meaning, why did I write the book the way that I did? Long story short, I wanted to give students something that they would actually read. This meant that it couldn't be too long, like a textbook, nor too boring, like, you guessed it, a textbook. I wanted it to be written in a familiar tone, with sound advice that people could easily relate to and make their own. And I wanted it to be real. I see this book as an older brother sitting down for a heart-to-heart with his 18-year-old know-it-all siblings. We're going to put it all out there – like the fact that you can and will catch a sexually transmitted disease if you're not careful, and that there are short cuts you can take when writing a paper, but using a 14-point font size ain't one of them.

The final point I want to make regarding the thoughts and energy put into this project is the rationale for my focus on *excellence*.

I've come across a number of study guides and academic resources billed as "survival" manuals. Survival, in my view, means just getting by, and that's simply not good enough. When you go to a nice restaurant, do you expect to be served a half-cooked pile of leftovers, or do you expect the five-star meal that you are paying for? Why then would you come to college and just want to survive? You're paying tuition, investing four years (or more) of your life, and planning on using this as a stepping-stone to bigger and better things. You need to do better than survive. You need to put yourself in the best position to get into the grad school of your choice, start your own business or get the job you want. You want to learn the most that you can, make valuable connections, and get the most out of your experiences.

I often think back to a classmate who said she was only going to study enough to get a "B" on an upcoming midterm exam. She went to bed while the rest of our study group continued studying. She ended up with a "C." Always push for the best, and never short yourself from the start. If you just want to get by, why do it? You can do better than that. But you must prepare for excellence in order to attain it. Keep reading, and I'll show you how.

TWO. WHO AM I?

Whenever I go to a presentation or hear someone give a talk, I usually want to know more about the speaker. What makes them qualified to speak on the topic at-hand? What have they done? Who are they? The same is true with books, especially non-fiction, "how to" books. What are the author's credentials? What makes them think they're smart enough to tell me what to do?

I'm sure some of you are sitting there right now thinking the same thing about me, so I'm going to take a few pages to let you know who I am and where I'm coming from. Hopefully this will give you a bigger picture of the experiences that led me to this project.

I'm an "80's kid," born and raised in a relatively small city (Harrisburg, Pennsylvania) in a two-parent, middle-class home, with my younger brother. We both attended public school where the student population was about 25% African American. My folks were from the old school, placing high value on education and hard work. In our house, you were expected to bring some homework with you each night and to stay on the honor roll, so early on, I had a goal-oriented mindset and confidence in my skills. When I struggled with something, my parents were there to help me, or encouraged me to seek outside assistance when it was beyond their scope…like when I had to stay after school a few times a week to get through Calculus in my senior year of high school.

I had a fairly typical high school life. I was well-liked, but pretty quiet back then. I had big dreams of leading the basketball team to the State Championships, but most of my career was spent on the bench. I ran track for a couple of years and did relatively well. I held down a few part-time jobs and had a steady girlfriend for much of my senior year. Like many other kids in my school, a few of my high points included getting my driver's license, graduation, and then making the big move to college.

After going through the application process then sorting through the options, I happily accepted an offer to my first choice, the University of Pennsylvania, located in Philadelphia, to study Computer Science and Engineering. I was awarded a ROTC scholarship which required me to take some non-credit classes each semester, so I ended up graduating in four-and-a-half years, instead of four. This included at least one summer school class each summer (I took most of my sciences in the summer because I didn't like them, and knew I would do better if I could take them by themselves).

When I first got to Penn, I attended two orientation programs – the African American Studies Summer Institute and the Pre-Freshman Program. The first program worked with about twenty-five Black incoming freshmen for a week. The second lasted four weeks and was for first generation college students, athletes, and others, like me, who didn't get a perfect score on their SATs. Attending both of these programs shortened my senior year summer at home but tremendously boosted my confidence level and comfort at Penn. When the other freshmen arrived to campus in September for the first time, I had already been there for five weeks taking mini-classes, meeting people, attending workshops, and learning the ropes. As a direct result, my freshman year went very well.

Over the years in school, I experienced many highs and lows, as would be expected. My girlfriend from back home broke up with me (imagine that!) towards the end of my freshman year, which was a shocking blow, since she was my first real relationship. But I did what we all must do...I moved on. Academically, sophomore year was my worst, mainly due to a lack of focus, a huge case of over-confidence, and thinking that I didn't need any help when my grades started to slip. I got it together again junior year, and also became quite active in a number of organizations, including the National Society of Black Engineers (NSBE) and a high school tutoring program called Positive Images. I also held a couple of part-time jobs, one working in a computer lab, the other tutoring Penn freshmen in Calculus (those extra hours in high school paid off!)

Junior and senior years, I found myself in several leadership positions on campus – something that I wouldn't have imagined while in high school. I became president of NSBE, director of Positive Images, and active in a lot of the campus politics concerning Black students. Socially, I was in the mix, but I didn't overdo it. I wasn't at the party every week, but when I was, I was usually the DJ – another side gig I held. I was much more content to hang with a small group of friends, or play pick-up basketball, or stir up a deep discussion in my dormitory, the W.E.B. Du Bois College House. This four-floor building was dedicated to the appreciation of African American culture, and was also a tremendous help to my success in school, due to its family environment and support services. I loved it so much there, I stayed all four-and-a-half years.

Like many of my friends, college was one of the best times of my life. I loved the freedom, the 2 AM conversations, the never-ending quests for free food, the activities and events, the pressure of having two exams and a paper due in the same week, and daily afternoon naps. I loved the excitement of starting a new semester, taking new classes, and having a fresh start. I loved the sense of accomplishment and closure once the semester was over. I loved the people that I met – the good friends I made, the professors who influenced me, and the important connections I was able to look up later.

I did a lot of growing up in college and learned a lot about myself. I realized that, like my father, I wanted to do things right or not at all. I also wanted to do things *efficiently*. With my busy schedule, wasting time was not an option. I picked up quite a few time management tips along the way, which I've included in this book. It was also during college that I discovered things about myself that I wouldn't have dreamed of…like the fact that I could lead organizations, and that I was a teacher at heart, like my momma. And a writer.

Before graduation, I decided that the military lifestyle wasn't for me. Fortunately I was able to end my tour of duty by agreeing to gradually pay back my ROTC scholarship. So instead of joining the Navy fulltime after graduation, I got a computing support job at Penn, and went to graduate school part-time, earning my Masters in Secondary Education. During that time, I joined the residential staff at my old dormitory, mentoring students, preaching academic excellence, planning activities, and giving back wherever else I could. A year later I published my first novel (that I had started writing in my junior year of undergrad). Four years after that, I married my college sweetheart and we had our first child.

We all have a purpose in life, something that we feel like we are driven to do. Like many people, I'm still trying to narrow mine down, but I do know that whatever it is, teaching and helping people grow is at the core. I've designed and taught courses, from the junior high school level through college. I've mentored, coached, and counseled whenever I could, not because I had to, but because I wanted to. In fact, as a junior at Penn I was the lead writer and editor of an academic handbook for Black students on campus. We undertook that project out of concern for the current freshmen and future classes. If we could show them what we'd learned by our junior and senior years, then hopefully they wouldn't have to repeat our mistakes.

A few departments on campus helped us make photocopies, then we circulated the handbook to every Black student we could. Five years later, while I was a grad student, I updated the text and passed it around again. I had never written anything like that before, but I knew that it had to be done, just as I now know that this expanded edition must be done.

Three of my favorite Kwanzaa principles are *Imani*, meaning "Faith" (my wife's name), *Nia* (my daughter's name), which means "purpose," and *Kujichagulia*, which means "self-determination." These three things are what this book is about, and also what your academic career is about. As we move forward, this will become much clearer to you.

Enough about me. I will build on some of my experiences, using them as examples, later in the book. But now, let's move on to an even more crucial question...

THREE. WHO ARE YOU?

Identity is an extremely critical issue throughout your lifetime, and particularly in your collegiate years. It's also quite a complex one, so before we get deep into our discussion regarding the importance of having a positive identity on campus, let's first make sure that we're on the same page with what exactly our definition of identity is.

Identifying identity

Identity deals with how you view yourself and how others view you. It can and should be looked at from a number of focal points. For example, what role have your parents played in your development? What does your skin tone, religion, style of dress or hair say about you? What's your historical story – individual, family, and that of the racial group(s) in your family tree? What are your personal values or beliefs? How have your neighborhood, your school, your extended family, and your peer group helped to define you? What makes you *you*?

These are challenging but important questions to answer. But even after you grapple with them, what makes matters more confusing is the fact that who you think you are may not coincide with how other people perceive and define you.

For instance, I may see myself as an honest, law-abiding citizen, however, this view may not do me a bit of good when I'm being racially profiled by police officers on a drive through New Jersey, or when I'm trying to catch a cab in Manhattan.

So there are two angles working at all times – an inner view, or "the man/woman in the mirror," and an exterior view, which is the way the world sees you. Sometimes they'll match up. Sometimes they won't.

There are also a number of layers or lenses through which you can reference the issue of identity. We all have an **individual identity**, which makes us the unique person that we are. You might be an artist and a pet lover who enjoys long afternoon walks and can't start your morning without your newspaper and cup of tea. Next, there's your **racial identity**. How has being an African American shaped your personal views, and how do you believe others view you as a member of this group? Do you have a specific ethnic identity, or ties to any particular cultural groups, such as Nigerian, Jamaican, or Dominican that are key to your background? You can also have a **gender identity**, or a sexual orientation identity. The historical struggles of women throughout the world and the marginalization of the homosexual community yields unique experiences which play a role in shaping their identities. There are other abstractions of this theme, and alternative identity possibilities, but we'll primarily deal with individual and racial identities.

As Beverly Daniel Tatum discusses in her excellent book, *Why Are All the Black Kids Sitting Together in the Cafeteria*, members of majority, or dominant groups, may not have ever factored their group membership into their identity equation.[1] For example, a white male may not see race or gender as a major defining point because he hasn't consistently been the minority in a stressful racial situation, or had to wonder if people question his qualifications because of race, or internalized the feelings of being followed around by department store security guards. Nor has he been denied access to an exclusive country club due to his sex, or been the punchline of a tasteless locker room joke.

For African Americans, however, because we live in a racist society, racial identity is almost always a part of the picture. The exact degree, however, can vary greatly.

Some African Americans may choose to make their world as "colorless" as possible. They judge people on their character, not their skin tone, and expect the same treatment in return. They celebrate the diversity of their American heritage, and either know very little of their African roots or simply choose not to emphasize them. On the other end of the spectrum, you have African Americans who change their names to represent their connection to Africa, wear traditional African clothing, and are keenly aware of race at all times.

For many of us, our racial identity fluctuates somewhere in the middle, and can depend on a number of social, historical, and individual factors. How we feel about race can change day to day, and even be a cause for inner conflict. We may be proud to be an American citizen, and feel lucky to be in this country, especially when hearing the painful details of civil war in Sierra Leone and Liberia, poverty in Haiti, and the rampage of AIDS throughout South Africa. But the Rodney King verdict, or an exhibit on slavery, or the gunning down of young African American men by Cincinnati police officers, or the failure of the public school system for many inner city youth, or our own poverty and HIV/AIDS statistics can enrage us and make us deeply question this country's value system. Some days you may want to take up the cause and speak out against racial injustice, and other days you may not feel like being the spokesperson for the Black race. That's perfectly natural. The important thing is that you have a healthy concept of who you are, and use that as your foundation.

Black is, Black isn't

Historically, college has been a time of soul-searching and inner exploration, and specifically for African American students, it's often a time to contemplate what it means to be Black. From the Civil Rights marches and sit-ins to the demonstrations for establishing Black studies programs, African American college students have developed their collective racial identity through political and social activism, as well as by engaging in serious discussion and study on campus. Spike Lee's 1988 classic, *School Daze*, captured the Black collegiate experience in a way that had not been done before, bringing to center stage age-old struggles of complexion, "good" and "bad" hair, and activism versus the desire for upward social and economic mobility. Many of these issues are still argued today.

How do you define Blackness? Must you wear a natural hairstyle to be authentically Black? If you aim to work for a Fortune 500 company or live in the suburbs, will you be branded a "sell-out?" Why does the media still often associate Black with negativity (crime, drugs), or otherwise ignore us, and how does this affect you? How will being Black influence your experience on campus?

While there is no clear cut answer to "what is Black," prominent researchers and scholars have developed a concept of African-centered expressions based on traditional values and cultural practices which are still evident today. For example,

African Americans tend to put an emphasis on extended families. Many of us have folks we call "aunt" or "uncle" or "cousin" who aren't really our family members. Some of us were raised by or spent significant time with relatives other than our parents, and we also enjoy occasional family reunions, whether they be planned or impromptu. This relates to what Howard professor, author, and psychologist A. Wade Boykin calls our **Communalism,** or our connection to others which goes beyond the nuclear definition of family, our social nature, and our intrinsic social responsibilities.[2] Other African-centered traits which Boykin delineates include:

- **Spirituality** – We have a deep religious history which sustained us through the period of slavery and the Civil Rights struggle. No matter the religion we practice, if any at all, there is typically a regard for a power greater than us.
- **Harmony** – Harmony relates to the idea that things are connected, and that achieving balance in life is necessary for a healthy experience.
- **Movement** – Many traditional cultural celebrations, such as Carnival, incorporate dancing and rhythm. From African drum and dance, to church praise and worship teams, to double-dutch, to college step shows and performance arts, movement and rhythm are important aspects of our culture.
- **Verve** – Verve represents energy, spontaneity, and knowing that there's more than one "right" way.
- **Affect** – Affect deals with how we *feel* about things, in contrast to concerning ourselves only with thoughts.
- **Expressive Individualism** – This is all about trend-setting, from our various styles of hair, choices of clothing, artistic and creative expressions, and developing our own unique personalities and sense of self.
- **Oral Tradition** – From the proverbs and histories passed down by the village griots and elders, to Sunday sermons, to spoken word and hip-hop, we have historically told stories with style.

- **Social Time Perspective** – We all know that the party doesn't start until we get there, and doesn't end until we leave!

These are common threads and practices which tie us together, and to our rich history and heritage in Africa. We may not all exhibit these items on the same level or in the same way, but it is extremely important to acknowledge our cultural interconnectedness. Keeping this frame of reference in mind will help you dispel the stereotypes and myths that may be attributed to you. In other words, if you know and understand your own definition of Blackness, you'll be much less distracted and affected by someone else's misinterpretation.

When ignorance strikes

Nevertheless, there will undoubtedly be times when race comes into question. There could be extreme cases such as racial remarks being scrawled on a student's door, offensive comments made by drunken (or sober) white students, bomb threats to the predominantly Black dorm or student organization, racist articles or cartoons printed in the school newspaper, or incidents of police harassment and racial profiling of Black students. All of these things happened during my time on Penn's campus, and I'm sure occurred in many other places as well.

There are also more subtle examples, such as the insecurity a Black student may experience in a predominantly white classroom, especially when they question whether or not they're receiving fair treatment from the professor or other classmates. An example of this can be seen in what Stanford professor Claude Steele calls "stereotype threat." This essentially deals with the fear a Black student may have of being put in a situation where they may support a negative stereotype.[3] For instance, an African American student may be hesitant to raise his hand in class in fear of giving the wrong answer and having other students think, "that Black kid really isn't as smart as us." This can affect even the most talented students, because they put so much pressure on themselves to perform well.[4]

Self-Hate

Insecurities about race can also come from within. Due to

the perception that we live in a "white world," combined with the historical and contemporary mistreatment of people of color, not only in America, but worldwide, one could easily ask the question, "why us?" Why have we been the targets of so much hatred, violence, and injustice? Why must Black people go through so much? Why do so many Blacks do poorly in school, or drop out all together? You may even question why you had to be Black.

There have been studies conducted where Black children chose white dolls over Black ones, and theories of self-hatred proposed by white scholars and African Americans.[5] Many factors contributed to these phenomena, such as the exclusion of positive Black images in popular media, and the inaccurate application of Eurocentric values to the Black experience. While we can't change history, we can study it thoroughly, and learn from it. When we do, we'll see that *all* racial groups have had their high and low points. Though it may seem like we're always catching the short end of the stick, rest assured, other people have had their historical struggles as well, and our history has many shining moments.

Black and proud

Research shows that the way you view yourself as an African American can play a tremendous role in your success at school. The more aware you are of the positives in the Black experience, and the more that you are taught about and prepared for potential racist episodes, the better suited you are to overcome adversity and achieve success. If you view your racial identity in a negative light, you'll be subjecting yourself to a potentially frustrating experience, worse because it's coming from the inside. Your own foundation will come into question.

Sometimes it's hard enough to find someone to support and encourage you, so when you're not able to motivate yourself, the struggle becomes that much more difficult. You don't want to constantly question yourself, or spend time and energy worrying about what other people think of you. Further, you don't want to buy into a mindset of failure, thinking that you really don't belong, or that affirmative action was the only reason you made it. The reality is that you're here. You're in school. And you have the opportunity to accomplish whatever you want, not to prove other people wrong, but to prove yourself right.

To become truly empowered, it is important to educate yourself on Black history, filling in the gaps that your earlier schooling may have left. You can do this through personal study or by taking African American studies courses on campus. A reading list is included on the book's website to help you get started (www.lionsstory.org/college). You can also participate in cultural, social, community, or political groups, and informally discuss current events and other critical issues with friends. It's essential to develop a support group that you can turn to on campus – peers, mentors, faculty and administrative contacts, advisors, etc. Equally important is understanding and applying the items outlined earlier, such as Spirituality and Expressive Individualism. These themes will help you explore Blackness on a variety of levels, celebrating the unifying traits but also appreciating the underlying differences throughout our culture.

African Americans are not a monolithic group. There are varying political and social views, different cultural philosophies and historical interpretations, variances in economic and social class, and opposing schools of thought on virtually any and every topic one can name. One side will choose Biggie, another Pac, while a small contingency of old school heads will argue for Rakim, and the new hip-hop era will push for Jay Z or Nas. This argument will go on forever. Further, we do not all like fried chicken and we're not all good dancers. And as the Williams sisters and Tiger Woods have shown the world, we *do* play tennis and golf. History has presented many obstacles, but as we collectively move forward, keeping in mind and spirit the determination of our ancestors to survive against the odds, we are persevering and excelling in all areas, without limits.

Other challenges

We all have a unique background and specific stories to tell, however, for many of us, there are issues in our past, or even still in our present, that are difficult for us. For example, students coming from a mixed racial background may have struggled to figure out how to blend both sides of their heritage and fit in with others. Or students who grew up wearing hand-me-downs and don't have loads of material items to bring with them to college may feel insecure around other students who come from money and have all of the latest expensive things.

How will people accept you? Will you have to "choose sides?" Will you be able to create a comfortable space to share your story? These are all very relevant questions.

The Bottom Line: Be Yourself

No matter if you're from a multi-racial background, African American, Caribbean, from the mid-west, south, old money or no money, you've been accepted into college and are about to embark on an exciting stage of life because of who you are and the things that you've accomplished. We've all struggled with identity issues, and will continue to face questions and challenges. What matters most is that we make healthy decisions, staying focused on what's gotten us this far, and where we have left to go on our personal journeys.

It's likely that when you step on campus for the first time as an incoming freshman, no one will know who you are. Some may not even truly know themselves. We've all heard the clichéd joke about college being the time for young adults to "find themselves." Yes, college certainly offers a tremendous opportunity for personal re-invention, but it's not required, nor is it necessary.

Just as back in high school, you might be tempted to alter your personal behavior in order to fit into a crowd or to fulfill some notion you had about what it means to be a college student. I remember a group of African American males at Penn who had been afforded the opportunity to attend some of the best prep high schools in America, but arrived on campus only to downplay academic success, party, and promote a host of negative stereotypes. We called them "Boarding School Thugs."

Perhaps they were afraid of change, or secretly questioned their academic capabilities and acted out as a way of coping with this stress. It could have also been that instead of falling victim to stereotype threat, they chose to *become* the stereotype because they perceived it as "cool." Or maybe they really just wanted to fit in and be accepted, no matter the cost. Either way, they were playing a dangerous game.

Some suffered academically, while others ultimately felt like outsiders socially and failed to really establish a connection on campus. Those that did link up with a mentor, or join an activity or organization, typically turned their experiences around. Others, sadly, fell through the cracks.

If you enjoyed playing the piano or basketball before you arrived on campus, there's no need to give them up. If you liked to read for pleasure, continue it when you have the time. If you're a people person, go out and introduce yourself. If you're more reserved, watch from the sidelines until you feel comfortable. Move at your own pace and explore the areas that interest you.

Everyone is going to be a little nervous the first day they get there, but you all are going to want pretty much the same things – to meet some interesting people, figure out where the dining hall is, and put off thinking about the first day of classes as long as possible. If you're genuine with the people you meet, you'll grow to develop genuine friendships. And over your collegiate career, as you take different classes, get to know different people, get involved in organizations, and pursue new interests and goals, you're going to change and mature. This will happen naturally, so there's no need to force it. Just be yourself and let those around you benefit from all that you have to offer.

FOUR. WHAT DO YOU WANT?

If you don't know where you're going, anywhere you end up will seem fine.

When you graduated from high school, you had options. You could have gotten a job, joined the military, or stayed at home. But you chose to go to college. Why? What do you hope to accomplish?

You may not have ever given this question much thought. Maybe you came to college because your parents wouldn't let you sit around watching TV all day. Or maybe you always knew you wanted to go to college, but you didn't really know why. You just knew that this was the next logical step after high school.

On the flipside, maybe you do know what you want. You might have dreams of going to law school, or being a graphic designer, or becoming a marketing executive, and you know that college is the ticket to achieving your goals. Or perhaps you have an interest in archeology, literature, or chemistry and want to continue your studies, eventually figuring out where this will lead you.

Establishing a connection

Whatever your reason for choosing college, it's important that you have one. If you don't know why you're here and what you hope to get out of the experience, please spend some time thinking about it. This is not to say that as a freshmen, you have to know what major you want to pursue. That's an important decision, and can be a difficult one, so take some time and figure out what's the best match for you. In the interim, however, you need to at least put yourself on the path to making your future vision clearer.

One way to do this is to identify a sense of purpose for your pursuits. Students may take a more serious approach to their academic career when they see it as serving a greater good.[1] Perhaps you want to give something back to your parents, siblings, or community. Or maybe your dream of becoming a doctor is rooted in the desire to work with Sickle Cell patients, or your entrepreneurial plans include establishing internships for inner-city youth. Obviously we all want to secure employment and opportunities that will allow us to pay our bills, put something away for later, and enjoy some of life's luxuries, but many of us also want to create social changes, big and small. Making money and making a difference aren't mutually exclusive. You can do both, and do them well.

From an African-centered perspective, the fact that you have the opportunity to attend college goes far beyond your individual accomplishments and abilities. You must take into consideration the efforts and sacrifices of people that you know, such as your family members who've struggled to provide the best for you. You must also consider the toils of people that you'll never meet, like those who fought against the "separate but equal" doctrine of the '50's, and our ancestors who were in bondage in this country but survived the harshest, most dehumanizing experiences possible. Whenever I get caught up in some personal issue or feel like I'm slipping off course from achieving a goal, I think about these things. I owe it to myself to make the most out of my opportunities, and I also owe those who came before me and paved the way.

Beyond academics and future career options, college also offers many extracurricular pursuits. Some of you may have really come to college to play a sport, develop a performance art, or take a variety of classes and see what sparks your interest. Honestly, I can't be mad at that. When I think about my college career, some of my best memories are from the organizations I was a part of, classes that had nothing to do with my major, and many of the lighter moments with the people I met.

I didn't really know what I wanted to do when I got to college. I chose to study computers based on the hunch that I'd probably like it, and the fact that I was good at math and "techy" type stuff. I ended up enjoying computers enough to finish my degree, but not enough to want to establish a hardcore technical career. In grad school I changed my focus to education, but I continued to use my computing background quite a bit in various capacities. Still, while in school, it was the broader appeal of the college lifestyle that kept me connected to the campus and motivated me to stay. I knew that I had to stay on top of my academics, and I took pride in my work, but I also recognize that if I hadn't been an active part of a few campus organizations, or took advantage of the other things college had to offer, my overall experience would have been much more difficult.

Setting goals

One of the keys to figuring out what you want is to set goals for yourself. And the first goal that you need to set once you step on campus is that you will leave with a degree. Don't assume that graduation is automatic, because the statistics say that this is far from the case. It's very easy to get caught up in the fact that you made it to college and that you're entering one of the most exciting phases of your life, however, you must not lose sight of the end goal. As the elders would say, *you've gotta keep your eyes on the prize*. Setting a goal to graduate will cause you to make a plan. Making a plan will bring you closer to creating a reality in which you're walking down the aisle with your diploma in hand.

Keep it real

We're going to get into the details of goal-setting and planning when we move to the Time Management section, but one thing that's important to mention now is that your goals must be realistic. Don't set yourself up for failure by trying to tackle "Mission Impossible." Suppose you didn't start out your college career with the best grades. Set some simple goals to improve, perhaps from a "C" to a "B," then map out a plan so that you can make this happen.

Now, if you're paying attention, this may sound like it contradicts something I said earlier, about a friend of mine shooting for a "B" instead of an "A" on an exam. It's a little more complex than that, so let's break it down.

If you've never typed before, it's not reasonable for you to plan on typing 60 words per minute after your first typing lesson. If you're training for a marathon, you're not going to begin with a 20-mile course. You need to pace yourself and set achievable goals, then continue pushing yourself forward. This builds confidence and a feeling of progress. If you aim too high you'll only end up frustrating yourself. Contrarily, when you know that you can do better and you aim low, like my friend did with her exam, then you're doing yourself a huge disservice, and you may miss out on an important opportunity as a direct result.

Another example of realistic goal-setting and planning would be to set a goal of improving your overall GPA, then register for three courses instead of four, focusing on classes where you know you can excel. Given this strategy, setting an "all A's" goal is reasonable because you feel confident in your abilities and you've reduced pressure on yourself by taking a lighter course load.

As we'll discuss in more detail later, your goals and your plan work hand-in-hand. You must decide what you want then figure out how to get it. Setting goals without creating a detailed and realistic plan can be summed up in one word – dreaming. It's okay to dream, but to reach your dreams, you have to map out what you need to do and then make sure it gets done.

You've gotta believe

After you establish your goals and iron out your plan, the next and most important step is to *believe in them*. Ultimately, this forces you to be real with yourself.

For example, suppose at the top of your goal list is "Graduate in 4 years and be prepared for medical school," but after a few semesters of undergraduate, and some poor performances in your science courses, that goal no longer seems so reachable. Was it really *your* goal to begin with? Many students think they want to be doctors because of the projected salary, the prestige of the position, or the fact that they haven't been exposed to other possible career choices in the health profession, or in something completely different. Parents or other influential people can also push you into pursuing a certain career, when you really have little or no interest in that choice.

If the goal is not in your heart, if it's not something that you want to do, then it will be that much harder to accomplish. The earlier you realize that, the happier you will be in the long run. Your goals must be about you. You have to believe that you will achieve them. If you truly want to be a doctor, your conviction will be the force that helps you overcome any obstacles, such as a poor early academic focus. You can excel after a slow start, but only if you believe in what you're doing and are passionate enough to work doubly hard, retake courses if necessary, and push a side door open if the front door is closed.

The importance of believing in your goals and your capabilities can not be understated, as self-confidence plays a key role in virtually every aspect of your academic career. According to Cynthia and Drew Johnson, authors of *Kaplan Learning Power*, **95% of school success depends on motivation, time management, and confidence.**[2] Does this mean that you can succeed by attending zero classes, turning in late homework, cramming for exams, but believing with 95% of your mind, heart, and soul that you will get an "A?" Nope. It simply doesn't work like that.

What this statement does tell us, however, is that a confident student will be secure enough to do a thorough self-analysis of their study skills, improve weaknesses, and use all of the resources available to them, while self-doubting students may feel so insecure about themselves that they won't seek help. A confident student will master the tricks of the trade and be self-aware that she has mastered these aspects, thus reaffirming her confidence. In other words, a confident student knows they've got it together, or will quickly find out what they need to do to get it together, and that reduces any apprehensions they may feel about their academic performance. Even if they hit a bump in the road, as we all do, their confidence will help them learn from their mistakes and move forward, instead of retreating or quitting all together.

Sometimes, we let our anxieties and nervousness tell us that something is too difficult before we've even given it a try. College is a perfect example. You hear about how different it is, or how a certain class or professor is almost impossible to pass, and you walk in the door with a whole bunch of self-doubt. Many African American students often secretly wonder to themselves whether they should even be there, with thoughts such as "I didn't go to the same high schools that these white kids went to. How can I compete with them?" Then there's always that one smart kid in class who answers every question as if he and the professor hang out together, and it makes you feel like you don't belong. But guess what? If you're in the room, then you do belong.

Don't worry about other people. It's not about them. It's about you, and what you want. Most of them aren't any smarter than you any way. Forty-one percent of white college students nationwide don't complete their degree after 6 years – this includes the ones that went to the best boarding schools in the country. They fail to finish for the same reasons everyone else does – not due to intelligence, but a lack of support, focus, and follow-through. So the real question becomes, "What are *you* going to do to make sure that *you* make it?"

Confident students know what they want, or know that they're on their way to figuring it out, then they put themselves in the best positions to succeed. They don't let fear or doubt steer them astray, not even a fear of success. As Nelson Mandela said, "Our greatest fear is not that we're inadequate. Our greatest fear is that we're powerful beyond measure." You must tackle that fear head-on by setting your goals, planning how to reach them, then following the plan, using every available resource along the way. The next section of this book will show you how.

PART TWO: IN THE CLASSROOM

FIVE. A DIFFERENT WORLD

Back in the late '80's, when Bill Cosby's Huxtables were the first family of primetime television, Denise left for a fictitious historically Black college on her own spin-off, aptly called *A Different World*. As Denise soon found out, and you will too, college truly is a different environment than what you're used to, and these differences stretch far beyond replacing Mom's home-cooking with cafeteria food. The items below are some key changes that you'll be faced with.

Semesters

Most college courses are on a semester schedule (Fall Semester, Spring Semester). Each semester or term typically lasts about twelve or thirteen weeks. Many colleges also offer two optional summer sessions which are usually condensed, lasting about six weeks each.

Some schools operate on a different timetable, such as a trimester schedule (Fall, Winter, Spring). The important thing to remember about semesters is they go by very quickly. In high school, most of your courses lasted the whole year. In college you have a much shorter time span to work with.

Professors

Teachers teach. Professors profess. This was a little saying that came to me after I experienced one of the worst professors ever in my freshman year Calculus course. Before that class, I imagined that every college professor would be a great teacher, because, after all, this was college. I thought they'd be the best since they were preparing us to be the future scholars and leaders of the world. I came to find out that college professors are often not hired for their teaching capabilities, but for their excellent research reputations, or their ability to churn out scholarly books.

For many professors, especially at large, research-driven universities, teaching is not their primary focus, so they may not be that good at it. They also may not be very accessible. More often than not you have to take deliberate steps to seek them out. Remember that high school teacher who kept you after class and told you to straighten your act up? That's a rarity in college. This is not the case everywhere, however. Excellent teaching and strong student-faculty relationships are the hallmarks of smaller institutions, and even smaller departments within larger schools. And some world-renowned researchers at large universities actually do make great teachers.

Campus Size and Environment

Some high schools may refer to themselves as "campuses" and have several buildings on a few acres of land, but in college, this is the rule rather than the exception. Instead of traveling down the hallway and stopping at your locker, you'll be traveling down the road, maybe stopping back at your dorm, cafeteria, library, or Student Center along the way. Some campuses are so large that they have their own bus service to shuttle students around. And large universities that have a graduate student program and their own hospital or research centers, in addition to their undergraduate students, can have tens of thousands of students and employees on campus daily. That's a long line at the bookstore!

On the flipside, there are tiny colleges across the country, or schools in small "college towns" which could be a huge culture shock if you're coming from "the big city." Whether you're moving across the country or only a few miles away to go to school, there's going to be an adjustment period as you settle into the campus culture and surroundings.

Class Size

I was part of a class once that had four students. I've been in others the size of a large theater, where almost every seat was filled. I've even heard of classes being so big that some students had to watch on TV monitors in a second location because they all couldn't fit in the main room. Unfortunately for freshmen at bigger schools, many of your introductory classes tend to be large, with 100 students or more. Larger classes, and even 10-person seminar courses, can be a major adjustment for someone used to twenty-five or thirty other high school classmates.

Class Times

Some classes may meet once a week for a few hours, some two or three times, for as little as fifty minutes each session. Rarely do you have a class that meets every day. Some classes, such as the sciences, have an additional lab and/or recitation (a class session to review material more in depth) that meets in a separate time slot from the lecture. These are often led by a Teacher's Assistant (TA). Classes can start at 8 or 9 AM, late morning, after lunch, in the late afternoon, or in the evening. Some schools even hold Saturday classes. Most likely, you will not have a continuous 8 AM - 3 PM course schedule like you did in high school. Your day will have gaps between classes, and some days, you may not have class at all.

Homework

You may be taking a college course that requires absolutely no outside work to be done. Other classes may only give reading assignments. Others, such as a math course, may resemble high school with weekly homework assignments due. The professor may or may not collect them, however. This often puzzles students, but in college, the purpose of a homework assignment may not be about getting a grade for completing it, but to give you practice in a particular area so that you're prepared for a future exam.

Midterms and Finals

In high school you may have had an exam at the end of each chapter or unit. In between exams, you probably had a smaller quiz or two. Most college courses that I've experienced (except foreign language classes) gave one or two midterms, and a final exam. "Midterms" are so-named because supposedly they come at the middle of the term (or semester), but I've had a midterm the day before a final. Sometimes your exams (midterms and finals) are cumulative, meaning that they cover *all* the material since day one of class. Sometimes exams just cover a specific amount of information. Some exams are standardized by the department, some are written by your professor. Some courses don't have any exams at all, but only consist of writing assignments, some sort of project, or a final presentation. Midterms and finals certainly raise the stakes in college, and reduce your margin of error. If you mess up, you may only get one more chance to come correct.

Grades

Most colleges use the 4.0 grading system, where a 4.0 is an "A," a 3.0 is a "B," and in between you have an "A-minus" (3.67) and a "B-plus" (3.33). (You can work out the rest on your own, but try not to see too many grades lower than a "B"). Some high schools use this system as well, while others, like mine, use the 100-point system.

Your high school grades were used to get you into college. You college grades will be used to get you into the rest of life – grad school, job choice, fellowships, etc. Once it's a part of your transcript, it ain't coming off, so don't let poor grades lock you out of good opportunities.

Credits and Requirements

Each course you take in college is worth a certain number of credits. Some schools call them "credit units," others "credit hours." Before you get your college degree, you need to earn a specific number of credits in particular areas. Depending on your school and your major, you may be required to take a well-rounded course load, with a certain amount of credits in a foreign language, writing courses, social sciences, etc. Your major will also outline specific courses you need to take each semester. For example, Economics majors can count on taking one or two Econ classes each term.

It's important to meet with your academic advisor or counselor periodically so that you make sure you're in the right classes and that you satisfy all of your graduation requirements. You don't want to have any surprises come senior year.

Academic Support

In high school, you may have never had the first thought about getting a tutor. You might even hold the misconception that getting a tutor is a sign of weakness, or only "dummies" need tutoring. Well, don't bring those thoughts to college. Smart people know that it's much better to have someone explain something to you, one-on-one, than wasting hours struggling with it on your own. Academic support tools such as extra help sessions, reviews, tutoring, advising, and workshops on study skills, reading comprehension, and time management are offered in colleges for a reason. You need them!

Responsibility

The onus is on you in college. You're not going to be spoon-fed answers, and the road to learning is not always going to be easy. You're expected to struggle with some difficult concepts. Through that experience, the hope is that you will truly learn how to process information, and why things work, rather than just memorizing facts. But again, what you get from college will be up to you.

Freedom and Flexibility

Ah, the two F's. These are the epitome of college. In high school you were on constant lockdown. You got detention for cutting class. You were on their schedule – they told you where to go, when to be there, and in some cases, what to wear. In college, you make your own rules. No one is going to come looking for you if you're not in class. No one is going to make you turn in your paper on time. Go ahead, sleep through your midterm. You won't get detention. But you just might get a third F, for *Failure!*

Summary

As you can see, there're quite a few new things to get used to. For some students, the adjustment may be difficult, because your high school routine is much more familiar. Whenever you move to a new job, however, you have to learn the ropes and meet new expectations. The same is true for college. You obviously have the talent and capability because you're here. You also have the desire, because you're still reading. So now you need to understand the skillset and strategies required for success, which we'll break down next.

SIX. LEARNING HOW TO LEARN: FIVE STEPS TO SUCCESS

Yeah, I know you've been in school virtually all of your life, and you think that you know what you're doing. But as I discussed in the previous chapter, you're about to enter a whole new ball game. As such, you're going to need to switch up your approach.

First, you need to **appreciate learning**. As a student, your job is to learn. And with any job, you want to achieve a certain level of job satisfaction. In other words, if you like what you're doing, chances are you'll do it well.

Secondly, you need to **take your education seriously**. You are the CEO of your academic career, the captain of your own ship. You're in control of how well you do. You can't half-step your way through this. You need to be willing to apply yourself, to put your time into it, and to want to achieve high results.

You may already have these two points covered, and if so, great. You're well on your way. If not, think about what you can do to adjust your outlook, because this is crucial to your well-being.

Now, let's move on to the actual study skills and techniques, by looking at **The Five-Step Formula for Success**.

The Five-Step Formula for Success

Step One: **Preview the material**
Step Two: **Get the most out of class**
Step Three: **Review the material shortly after class**
Step Four: **Study smart, not long**
Step Five: **Use your resources**

Doesn't seem too complex, does it? The steps themselves are common sense, but the application can be a little difficult, for a variety of reasons. In the rest of this chapter, we'll discuss each of the steps in detail, along with common obstacles that can hinder your progress, and how you can overcome them.

>> Step One: Preview Each Lesson

Of the five steps in the Formula for Success, Previewing the Lesson is probably the most overlooked. Many students go into the classroom with absolutely no idea of what's going to be covered. Some students don't think to preview the lesson, out of over-confidence or a failure to fully grasp the importance of this step. Others simply don't make the time. A lot of us think that we do better when we're "under the gun," meaning that without the pressure of an upcoming exam, we may not give much thought to serious studying. This was how I functioned in my early days of undergrad, mainly because I didn't know any better. Eventually, however, the demands of my Engineering courses made me adjust my methods and I started incorporating more lesson previewing techniques.

Each time a professor steps into a classroom to teach, they have an agenda and a plan. Instead of just showing up and sitting there, you also need to enter the classroom with an agenda and know specifically what you want to get out of the class session. There are several approaches to this, some in-depth and others quite simple, but the overall objective is to give you a head start in the class. Essentially you can think of it as looking at a roadmap before setting out on a trip to an unfamiliar area. You do like to know where you're going, right? I thought so. Let's check out some previewing techniques then talk further about why they are essential.

Using the syllabus

Most college courses will provide you with a syllabus outlining weekly topics that will be covered in class, reading assignments, important due dates, and other pertinent course info. The more detailed the syllabus is, the better off you'll be. A good syllabus will break a 500-page course textbook down into the 200 pages that you actually need to read, and will give you a decent outline of the course material, including a list of important topics and key words.

You'll want to spend some time going through the syllabus. Look over it entirely when you first get it so that you can understand the scope of the course. Don't simply tuck it away in a folder, and never toss it in the trash. In the most basic form of previewing a lesson, you'll check the syllabus before each class to see what topic the professor is going to cover. This takes all of 30 seconds but at least will let you know what to expect in class that day.

Reviewing previous material

Before you go to class, either the night before or the day of the class, take 10-20 minutes to review the notes from the previous lecture, as well as the reading and any notes you took from it. This will get you mentally prepared for the upcoming class session. Take note of any concepts or terms you didn't understand, or other questions you have for the professor, and ask these points during or immediately after class. Don't plan on doing this step *during* class because then you won't be able to fully focus on the class discussion.

Reading ahead

There's no rule that says you can't look ahead to next week's reading right now. Think about how excited we are to hear music before it's released or get a sneak preview of a movie before it hits theaters nationwide. But when it comes to the books, we have the hardest time staying caught up. This is because most of us don't even think about looking ahead. Plan on completing each week's reading assignment, then at least scanning through the next one. This will give you a taste of the information, which will help you the second time around when you sit down to read it through carefully.

Moving ahead (previewing the entire course)

I had a pre-med friend in college who would stay at least two or three chapters ahead of the rest of the class in her science courses. She would actually do the readings and the problem sets as if they were due, then once the class caught up to her, she would redo them, filling in any concepts she didn't get the first time around. For her, this wasn't an overburden or a lot of extra work, but her strategy for staying on top of her classes. Needless to say, she did quite well and got into the medical school of her choice.

Auditing a course

This is another technique for previewing an entire course which can be extremely useful if you have the time to do it. Basically you'd be sitting in on the class without actually receiving a grade for it. Some schools will let you register for the course under the "audit" option, or you may have to skip the registration and just go to the classes, either because you've already enrolled in your max course load or you're not able to audit courses. Either way, it's good to let the professor know that you're there. How in depth you go in the course is really up to you. You may just want to sit in on the classes to get a feel for the material or you may want to actually work through the assignments as if you were a part of the class. The professor may even let you take the exams.

This is a great way to deal with a more difficult course or one that you have reservations about taking. Sitting in will give you a good idea of the content and hopefully ease your fears.

Summary

No matter the approach, previewing the lesson should help you build your confidence and keep you focused on the course material. By staying familiarized with the syllabus you'll be able to see if the professor is moving faster or slower through the weekly breakdown, which could have implications on your exams and other assignments. The preview is a vital first look that will make your subsequent study of the material more efficient and effective. If utilized on a regular basis, previewing can not only keep you caught up in class, but ahead, which is where you want to be.

>> Step 2: Get the most of out class

Before we get into the whats and hows, let's look at a few scenarios...

Scenario One: You're a freshman, and either because you didn't have many options or you felt inclined to make your college schedule look like high school, you've signed up for classes Monday, Wednesday, and Friday starting at 9, 10, and 11 AM. Things go well for about a month, until the first batch of midterms. You've pulled a few all-nighters to cram for your exams and finish a paper. Around the same time, you and a new "special friend" have been keeping late nights. The evening rehearsals for the a cappella group you joined have been getting longer too, in preparation for the big show coming up. Suddenly you're a lot more tired than you used to be, and that 9 AM class isn't as easy to get to anymore. Neither is the 10 AM.

Scenario Two: You just got back your first midterm from your math course. You got a "C-minus." How could the professor give you that grade? Why did she make the test so hard? What kind of nonsense are they pulling here at this school? You're fed up. Luckily a friend tells you that her ex-boyfriend's roommate's frat brother had the same course last year and thought it was a waste of time. He stopped going to class after the first midterm and ended up with a "B-minus" in the course. Sounds like a plan.

Scenario Three: You make it to class a few minutes late, as usual. You ease into a seat in the back. The professor is way down in the front, writing some stuff on the board, talking about a new theory or something. You're still getting settled in, so you'll figure it out later. First, you've got to eat the muffin you grabbed on the way to class, then go over your "to do" list, then finish up your last few homework problems that you need to turn in for your afternoon class. Whatever this professor is talking about can't be all that important since the guy two seats down from you has fallen asleep.

Scenario Four: You're so proud of yourself. It took you until junior year, but you've finally got this college thing figured out.

Every semester you need to find at least one easy course to take (sometimes known as a "gut" class) so that you can count on one guaranteed "A" with minimal effort. Looks like you've picked a real winner this semester – there's only one paper due (3-5 pages...you can do that in your sleep), the final is multiple choice, and most of the readings are optional. You decide that attendance should be optional as well, so you pop in when it fits your schedule.

Any of these situations sound familiar? Wait, there's more. Skipping a class because you didn't finish a paper. Cutting out of town early for spring break. And my personal favorite, not going to the class after a midterm as a self-reward for getting through the test. Guess what? No matter what the excuse or rationale, skipping classes – whether you're physically absent or mentally absent – is not a good idea at all.

Attendance is Mandatory!
This is the first rule to getting the most out of class, because if you're not there, how are you going to get anything at all? For decades, this terrible rumor that class attendance isn't necessary has circulated through college campuses across the country. And then people wonder why they have a 1.57 GPA.

Here's why you need to be there:
- **You need to know what's going on**. Many professors, especially in large lectures, base a majority of their exam material on what's covered in class and the handouts they give, not the textbook.
- **You need to be a part of the discussion**. Some courses weigh class participation as part of the grade, especially smaller seminars. These are easy points to earn – all you have to do is show up and speak up.
- **You need the inside information**. Often before exams professors will really key in on exactly what will be tested. They may specify which chapters to pay careful attention to or even give you sample exam questions.
- **You need to see how to do it**. For classes involving computations (math, sciences, business, stat, engineering, and many others), you need to be there to see the professor step through example problems, then ask questions if there's

anything you don't understand. This can save you hours of wasted time trying to figure it out yourself.

- **You need a firsthand account**. If you miss class, how can another student explain to you in two minutes what happened over the course of fifty or more?

- **You need to be seen**. Even if a professor doesn't specifically state that they factor class attendance into your final grade, trust me, it matters. If a student struggled in a course but at least showed up and participated, that effort is generally taken into consideration when final grades are calculated. You have to make a good impression, though. Don't think you can sleep through the semester in the back of the room without the professor taking notice.

- **You need to recognize**. If you attend a predominantly white university and are in a predominantly white class, do you think the professor isn't going to take notice of your absence?

- **You need to establish relationships**. You should develop a good rapport with the professor, especially if this course is in your major or of specific interest to you. You don't have to become best buddies or think of it as brown-nosing, but if you want to be an accountant and your professor is an accountant teaching accounting, doesn't it make sense to connect with them? Who knows, they may write you a recommendation one day. You also need to network with your classmates to form study groups or at least have one or two people you can run questions by. If your class attendance is shaky, other students will likely avoid letting you into their study group for fear that you're not taking the course seriously.

- **You need to ask questions**. This is essential to your learning process because not everything is going to make sense the first time around. Professors want and expect questions, either during class or immediately before or after. This is part of the process, but if you don't show up, you miss out.

- **You need to use your time wisely.** Attending class is far more effective than wasting time hunting down a classmate, deciphering and copying their notes. You may spend twice as long going through this process, instead of actually using that time to begin studying the material.

Some classroom math

I'm a practical person by nature, so let's take a quick look at some numbers. Tuition at a top private college runs about

$30,000 a year. That's just tuition – no room and board, food, books, or other stuff. Just tuition. This breaks down to $15,000 for a semester. Most students take 4 or 5 classes per semester. Let's say this term, you're taking 4, so you're paying $3750 per course. Suppose one of your classes meets Monday, Wednesday, and Fridays for an hour. Over the 13-week semester, the course will meet about 37 times. So each time you don't show up, you've burned a Benjamin (that's $100 for all the broke folks in the back).

Don't pay the price

Okay, so maybe you don't care about the wasted tuition money if it's not coming directly out of your pocket. Here's something that you will take the hit on, however. Some courses penalize your grade if you miss too many classes. This will be explained to you on the first day of class, and will typically be clearly spelled out in the course syllabus as well. Don't be stupid and have your grade lowered by not showing up. You may not be able to control how hard the exam is, but you can certainly control whether or not you show up for class. Everyone can and should get an "A" in attendance.

What if you really *must* miss a class?

There are legitimate reasons for missing a class. Those reasons are the same as missing work or another important engagement – illness, travel that can't be rescheduled, or some other emergency. When you miss work, what should you do? You call out. The same goes for class.

If you know in advance that you have to be out of town, let the professor know beforehand. They'll respect this act of common courtesy. Ask for any handouts, notes, or assignments. If you have an emergency that day, or are ill, send the professor an e-mail or voicemail as soon as you're able to. This is especially true for smaller courses, although don't think that just because a course is large that you can skip it when you want to sleep in. With freedom and independence comes responsibility. Abusing your freedom is only going to hurt you in the long run, so act like you know, and get to class!

Now that you've made it to class, what's next?

Sit down and pay attention. No, seriously. What you need to do is *sit down and pay attention* in class, otherwise, there's no point for you being there. You'll do this by being an **active participant** and **taking useful notes**. Let's discuss each of these so you can see how they're done.

Active listening and participation

Think of class as a conversation. Yes, often the professor will be the only one doing the real talking, but that's only a small piece of the puzzle. The real conversation should be going on inside of your head. Think about what the professor just said – does it relate to something he or she said earlier, does it make sense, do you understand it? How can you apply it to the reading that you did before class or the problem set that's due next week? How does it relate to the upcoming exam? If the professor poses a question to the class, answer it in your head, or maybe even jot down some notes. As the professor talks about different ideas and concepts, turn those into questions as well. This is how you generate the classroom conversation, and how you remain engaged and attentive.

It's very easy to remove yourself from the equation by sitting back and letting your mind wander off. When you do this, you may hear what's going on in the background, but you're not really *listening*. By thinking about what's going on during class, you'll stay more alert and retain more of the information.

The Benefits of Active Listening.

- **Better notes.** You know what to write down and what not to write (this will be explained more in the next section).
- **Better retention.** You'll remember more of what was covered in class because it didn't just pass through your ears, but was also processed by your brain.
- **Better comprehension.** The material should make more sense to you because your attention span isn't fading in and out. Many times confusion sets in not because the material is difficult, but because you weren't really listening.
- **Better questions.** Not everything is going to sink in right away, but by paying attention you'll immediately know when

you don't understand something and can write your question down in your notebook.

- **More productive study sessions.** Instead of leaving class and having to figure out the material on your own at home, you should have a pretty good idea of the major points right after class. You still have to struggle with the concepts and work through applying the theories to specific problems or questions, but you'll be much more prepared.

How Do You Become an Active Listener?

- **Do the prep work.** If you've previewed the day's lesson, it should be more interesting to follow along. Plus, if you came up with some questions during your preview, you'll want to pay attention to the lecture to see if any of your questions are answered during class.
- **Focus.** Imagine that the professor is talking directly to you. Stop thinking about what you're going to do the rest of the day and pay attention to what's going on.
- **Minimize distractions.** Don't come to class thinking that you're going to work on homework for another class, or play your GameBoy, or hold a quiet conversation with your neighbor, or stare at that good-looking classmate two rows up.
- **Check yourself.** There are going to be moments when you start slipping. You might feel sleepy, or your thoughts may drift. Get it together and get back on track.
- **Rest up beforehand.** If you go to class sleepy, guess what? You're probably going to fall asleep. If you've ever been sleep-deprived like I've been, you know that you can drop pretty much anywhere. I've fallen asleep in movies, at church, when visiting friends, when having friends visit me, in the bathtub, on the floor, on waiting room sofas, in passenger seats, and in the front, middle, and back of my fair share of classrooms (I'm not condoning it, I'm just saying that it happened). When you're really tired, you won't be able to control that nodding off feeling, nor will you be able to really focus on the lecture. We'll talk about this more in the Time Management section, but try to get on a regular sleeping schedule, and go to class well-rested...especially if you're a snorer.

Taking useful notes

Your notes have a purpose. They're to help you capture important moments from class so that when you sit down to study, you'll have an easier time recalling and comprehending information. Many students, however, don't know how to take effective class notes, nor do they understand that they need to review their notes *early* and *often*, so they fail to take full advantage of this essential learning tool.

There are a few note-taking strategies and methods that you can try. I'll outline two effective ones in a moment. First, let's talk about some **common mistakes that students make when taking notes.**

- **Taking Dictation.** You're not a secretary, so there's absolutely no need to record word-for-word everything that comes out of your professor's mouth. You'll find that some professors like to tell stories that really have nothing to do with the lesson. And let's be real – if you're busy jotting down every word, are you really listening and thinking about what's being said? And are you going to go back and read through all 20 pages of your notes? Do you realize how huge your notebook is going to be at the end of the semester?

- **What is this?** If you can't read your own notes, how are they going to help you?

- **Second-hand shorthand.** It's great to abbreviate and take short-cuts (we'll talk about this in a second), but if you're using someone else's symbols or making them up as you go along, you're going to spend more time figuring out what your notes actually mean, and not studying them.

- **Color-Coding.** It may look fabulous to have all of your definitions in lavender ink and example problems in navy blue, but who has time for that? You're going to miss important information while you switch to the correct pen color. If you must, save this for your second batch of notes (see below).

- **Smudgeville, USA.** Use a basic ball point pen with ink that doesn't bleed through the page. Pencils, felt markers, and even some gel ink pens can make for a messy situation.

- **What notes?** You might take decent class notes but if you never look at them again until the day before an exam you're not really using them to your best advantage.

- **Wrong Class!** If you're in a discussion-based course, you probably won't need to take a whole lot of notes. The keys to these kinds of classes are listening and participation. Do keep a pen and paper handy to jot down important points in the discussion, such as a book title or author you want to check later, or a quote that you can use for a paper.

Note-taking Method One: The Cornell System (also known as the Two-Six Method)

Divide your paper into two columns – the left, called the Recall Column, about 2 or 2.5 inches wide, and the right, the Note-taking Column, taking up the remaining 6 inches of your paper. During class you'll jot down important ideas, definitions, example problems, etc. in the wider column. Shortly after class (as soon as you can make the time), review your notes, then *reduce* them in the left hand column. Write down key words or summary statements, connect ideas and jot down questions. After you've done this step, cover up the larger side with a sheet of paper, look at the Recall Column and quiz yourself on what you remember by looking at the key words and questions you've recorded.

Note-taking Method Two: "Notes" notes

Go to class and take your notes as usual. Shortly after class (again, as soon as you can make the time – the sooner, the better), read through your notes, then re-write them. Your re-write will be a neater, more organized version. It allows you to color code material or type up your notes, if this is your thing, because you can move at your own pace. You can also reword your notes more clearly, cut out unnecessary stuff, and re-group certain facts or statements if it makes sense to do so.

Comparing the two methods

First of all, notice that both methods require you to look at your notes immediately after class. We'll talk about this more in Step 3 (Review), but clearly, notes aren't meant to be recorded then pushed to the side. The Cornell Method is cool because essentially, you're taking notes only once. With "notes" notes, you'll spend extra time re-writing your notes, but for some students, or for some courses, this may work better for you. It's not necessarily time wasted because you are working with the material, letting it sink into your head. But some people would prefer not to do their entire notebook twice, which is understandable.

Honestly, though I'm familiar with the Cornell system, I don't know many people who use it – at least not in its full format. I think it may have something to do with the fact that people aren't used to splitting their paper into columns. When I looked back at some of my old notes, however, I realized that even though I didn't divide my pages, I was squeezing summary statements and questions in the left hand margin, because they were easier to quickly read through there. I also do this in books, because it's faster to skim through and find my summary statements and notations, instead of having to read all of the text again. The summary statements or questions are usually enough to trigger the memory and remind you about what was recorded in the larger column, which, in my opinion, makes the Cornell system worth a try…even if dividing your paper into columns seems like an awkward idea.

What to write

Regardless of which method you choose, or whether you develop your own note-taking style, you need to know what to capture from class. Some students write too much, others too little. I can't really give you a rule of thumb (ie, for a one hour class you should have 5 pages of notes), because each course and each teacher is different. You need to pay close attention and be able to decipher what's worth writing down. Here are some keys:

- **The Date.** That's a great place to start. Dating each page of your notes helps you keep them organized.
- **Example problems.** These are crucial for classes like math, sciences, statistics, and others. Don't just copy them down, though. Listen, learn, and write. Your ability to comprehend these examples will be key when you're working through homework problems, and later on, exam questions.
- **Stuff from the board or overhead.** If the professor takes the time to jot something down or show a specific slide, it will usually contain some important content. You don't have to necessarily copy it down exactly as they did, though. Think about it, and record it in a way that makes sense to you.
- **Definitions, Terms, Formulas, and Theories.** Many times these will fall under the category of "Stuff from the board

or overhead," but some professors will just recite them out loud, so pay attention.

- **"You'll be tested on this."** Anytime you hear those words (and a lot of professors really do come right out and tell you), start writing!
- **Questions.** During lecture, if something is discussed that you don't quite understand, write your question down.
- **Summary.** For some students it helps to sit for a few moments after class and write a short (2-4 sentence) summary of what was covered. What were the important points? What's still a little fuzzy? What should you be sure to look at when you study?

How to write

Below are some quick tips to help you efficiently record your notes.

- **Use loose leaf.** Store your notes in a three ring binder. This allows you to use as much or as little paper as you need, and if you want, you only have to carry around paper, not your whole binder. Some of you might be partial to spiral notebooks, or your mom might be a lawyer and have the hook-up on legal pads. If it works for you, stick with it.
- **Use a ballpoint pen.** It's neater and won't bleed. Carry around a spare or two in case you run out of ink.
- **Use phrases.** No need for complete sentences. Just the key words. Short and sweet (which is less to read through later!)
- **Use abbreviations.** As you take more notes, you'll develop your own natural style for abbreviation. For example, I took a lot of African American studies courses, so instead of writing "African American" every time it was mentioned in class (which was a lot), I wrote "Afam." I also picked up some standard shorthand, such as "b/c" for *because*, "w/" for *with*, and "w/o" for *without*. Finally, because of my math and engineering background, I used a lot of symbols, such as "≈" for *approximately* and "≠" for *not equal*. Whatever abbreviations you use, make sure that they make sense to you.
- **Skip spaces.** I haven't heard about a worldwide paper shortage, so there's no need to crowd everything together. Skip a few lines here and there in case you need to add something in later. It's also easier on the eyes. Additionally,

you may want to start each day's notes on the top of a new page.

What if the professor provides handouts?

Some professors have their own notes that they make available to you via handout or online. Sometimes these notes will be the basis of the class lecture and other times they'll be a side reference that may not be used an awful lot. Having these handouts doesn't mean that you don't have to take notes, however. If the professor uses them in class, bring them with you and write down questions and comments in the margin, or on a separate piece of paper if need be. If the handouts are more of a reference, and not a central class tool, review them and hold on to them in case you need them for a future assignment or to prepare for an exam.

Tape recording classes

Some students feel the need to record classes, either via a small audio tape recorder or even with a video camera. In my opinion, if you're going to go do this, there needs to be a purpose. Is there a special guest speaker that you want to capture? Are you writing a paper and want to pull out exact quotes from the class discussion? If you're just recording a class in lieu of taking notes, you may not be benefiting yourself much. Will you actually listen to the tapes (and do you realize how much time this takes)? Are you getting anything useful from them? Hey, if you do, and it works for you, then by all means, do your thing. Make sure to have extra batteries and a spare blank tape so you don't miss anything. But if you're recording classes and not doing anything with the tapes, save yourself the trouble and just stick with the good ol' notebook and pen.

Notes on your laptop

Laptop computers have become a big thing, and are gaining popularity now that wireless internet is more widely available. While it's typically more efficient to rely on paper and pen to take class notes, you may feel more comfortable typing them up on your laptop. If so, make sure to carry around a pen and pad as a backup. Laptop batteries don't last forever (and die even quicker when you forget to charge them!). Also don't let your laptop be a distraction. When you're in class, avoid the internet, games, other class work, etc. If your laptop has sound, mute it during class. You don't want to catch a bunch of funny looks when your computer announces that "you've got mail" or your favorite CD is on auto-play. Finally, keep a close eye on your laptop. They're much easier to steal than desktop computers and typically more expensive to replace.

Don't trash them!

It's tempting at the end of a semester to do a clean sweep and dump all of your coursework into the incinerator. But if you're in Chemistry 1 now, guess what might come in handy in Chemistry 2? Put your old notes in a box somewhere, especially for courses in your major. But even those notes from an obscure elective may come in handy again, so hold on to them.

Note-taking Summary

Regardless of the method or style you use to take notes or the type of paper you write on, remember to write for a reason. Make sure your notes mean something to you, and make sure you take a good look at them throughout the semester, not just at exam time.

Some Final Thoughts on Getting the Most of out Class

Where to sit?

I didn't cover this first, because honestly, it's not really that big of a deal. A lot of study guides will direct you to sit front and center so that you can see the professor clearly and he or she can see you. This also should help you stay awake, ideally. If you're really tired, however, you might doze off no matter where you're sitting. You know something else? Not everyone can sit in the front of the room. There simply aren't enough seats.

If you feel like sitting in the front, maybe to see better or because this helps you focus, get to class early and pick out your favorite spot. Otherwise, as long as you can see and hear clearly, anywhere in the room is fine, except the very back. There's really no good reason to sit all the way back there, except on the rare occasion that you have to leave early and don't want to disrupt the class.

When the bell rings

Okay, most campuses don't have bells, but if your class is scheduled to end at 11 AM, don't play "ready, set, go" at 10:58. First of all, a lot of professors will drop the most important information right at the end of class. Some may even keep you a few extra minutes so they can finish up. You might huff and puff because you're ready to leave, but even if you're mad, you better pay attention and keep your notebook out.

Secondly, instead of going off to lunch or playing video games, stick around after class for another five or ten minutes and ask your questions. This might save you a trip to office hours. One trick I used to do was to let other students ask their questions first, then eavesdrop. Sometimes they asked the same questions I had, and other times they would bring up stuff that I hadn't even thought of.

You don't have to ask questions every week or bust a brain cell trying to think of a reason to see the professor after class. Chances are, if you've put your time into studying, you'll come across some points which could use further explanation. If you're really pressed for time and can't hang around, come early to class next time, or just go to office hours.

What if the class is really boring?

Let's be honest. Some classes are going to be a struggle to get through. Not every professor is going to be exciting and energetic, and not every course topic or lecture is going to be interesting. **You still need to be there**, for all of the reasons I previously stated. I will say, though, if you're really not getting a whole lot out of the class, then in the interest of time management, sit somewhere in the middle and listen with one ear while you do something else – study some other class notes, read through the text, outline a paper, or something constructive. Don't play around or fall asleep, though. That's not a good way to earn cool points with the person who'll be giving you your grade. Trust me, they will see you.

What if the class is absolutely pointless?

I added this question because it's a very valid one. Some students really do feel like sitting in the classroom is a complete waste of their time. If you find yourself thinking this way often, or pulling out other work to do in class every single time, or even skipping a lot of classes, then you really need to re-evaluate why you're enrolled in the course. If the subject is not interesting or you really don't connect with the professor, look into dropping the class and taking something else, or switching to a different instructor. If that's not an option, figure out some way to make this experience relevant to you. Your grade depends on it.

Summary

This was a lot of information. If you need to, read through it again so that all of the details sink in. And when you go into the classroom, have a positive attitude and a solid strategy for success, applying good note-taking and listening skills. The effectiveness of your study sessions relies on what you pulled from the classroom, so make sure that you get all that you can.

>> Step 3: Review shortly after class

This is another quick and easy step that often gets overlooked. Many times, once you leave Class A, your focus immediately shifts to Class B and C, an extracurricular activity, a job, or nothing at all. Immediately reviewing the material from Class A needs to be built into your studying process, before you move on to the next thing on your "to do" list.

Joy in repetition

The more times we see something, the more familiar it will become. Reviewing the material right after class gives you another chance to look it over. Since the class just ended, the information is fresh in your mind, however because you're now processing it on your own outside of the classroom, you may begin to look at it in a different way, or identify additional questions for the professor (or teaching assistant or tutor).

This is also a great opportunity to review the course notes you took to make sure that everything makes sense and that you follow the material. And since both note-taking methods I described in the previous section require you to review, you need to map out some time to follow through on this.

Finally, by working with the material one additional time, it should ease your serious studying quite a bit. Many times students have to cram for midterms and finals because they're trying to learn information that they've never seen before due to the fact that they 1) didn't do the reading, 2) didn't go to class, and 3) couldn't review for a class they didn't attend. If you can commit to a sound strategy of previewing the lesson, paying attention in class, then immediately reviewing the material after class, you will have been exposed to the information three times instead of none. Obviously, this makes a dramatic difference.

When and how to review
Ideally you would review immediately after the class, but for many students, this isn't possible due to other time commitments. If you can't carve out some time to do an immediate review, make it a point to look over the material again sometime before you go to sleep for the night. Once you've slept off the information, your review could become more like re-learning because the information is not as familiar.

The time it takes to do a decent review can range widely and depends on a number of factors. If not much went on in class that day, or you already feel pretty confident with the material, don't skip the review, but instead give 5-10 minutes to scan through the class notes you took. You don't want to cut the review step out because the idea is for you to get used to a study routine, incorporating all of the steps. When you get sometimesy with steps in the system, eventually you will completely fall off.

If you're using the "Notes" notes method (described earlier), or if there was a lot of material covered in class, your review session may take an hour or more. That's perfectly fine. Map out the time that you'll need so that you can get the job done. And pay attention to the next step which will give you pointers for maximizing your study sessions.

>> Step 4: Study smart, not long.

Studying is one of the more common words heard on college campuses. There are many activities which can fall under the realm of "studying" – your lesson preview and review, doing your assigned reading, preparing for an exam, writing a paper, doing research, working on a class project, meeting with a study group, doing a homework assignment or problem set, and more. Basically, any instance that you're spending time on your school work can be considered studying.

In most cases, outside of a group study session or meeting with a tutor, study time will be spent quietly going through your course text and notes. You're going to spend a lot of time doing this, so one of the first keys is to identify study locations where you feel comfortable and where you can get your work done.

Where to study

Notice in the previous paragraph, I said study *locations*, in the plural. You should frequent a few study spots in case one is not available (for instance, if your normal study lounge is crowded and noisy, it's good to have a backup choice). Also, when studying, sometimes the material can be so heavy that you need to change your scenery and reset.

When picking ideal study locations, consider the following:

- **Minimize distractions.** The more stuff that's going on around you, taking your attention away from your books, the less productive your studying will be. Distractions come in all flavors – TV, friends and roommates, music, video games, instant messaging and e-mail, to name a few. If you study in your room, be sure to establish some "quiet hours" or work out an arrangement that allows everyone in the room to coexist happily and take care of their needs. You also need to make an agreement with yourself – when you're studying, turn the ringer off, step away from the instant messaging, and do what you're supposed to be doing.
- **Useful workspace and resources.** Make sure your work area fits the job because this makes your work more efficient. If you're researching through a lot of books and notes, find a space that's not cramped, with a large table so that you can spread out. If you study in your room, set up an area that has

the supplies that you need so that when you sit down, you can get right into it and feel comfortable in your own space.

- **Not *too* comfortable, though.** Watch out for the soft lounge sofas or studying in your bed. You might wake up a few hours later with drool in your book.

- **Good lighting.** Remember your mother telling you not to strain your eyes by reading in the dark? Well, she was right. There's absolutely no good reason to study in a poorly-lit environment. I find that I'm much more alert and focused when I have good overhead lighting. This is especially useful when studying after a long day of classes. Dim lighting can be a quick invitation to drowsiness, which won't do anything for your memory retention. It also causes unnecessary eye strain which could give you a headache. Get a good desk lamp for your room, and when you study elsewhere, pick a spot that's nice and bright.

- **Convenience.** One of the great things about college is that there are so many places to study. Pick a good place near your classes, your job, or other areas on campus that you frequent. This will make it easy to squeeze in study time when you're between classes, work, activities, etc.

- **Try and see.** Do your reading in a coffee shop one day, sit outside in the grass, go to another dorm's lounge, or if you're school is in a cluster of colleges, check out one of the other campuses. If you find a place that works for you, stick with it.

- **The Library Lie.** I used to think that I'd do my basic studying in my room or the dorm lounge, then when it was time to get serious for a midterm, I'd move my operations to the library. Seems like everyone else had the same idea. You don't have to study in the library. There are plenty of other nice buildings on campus. A lot of schools leave their classrooms open, which make great study spots or group meeting locations. If the library's crowded, or just isn't your thing, find someplace else that's a better fit.

When to study

One of the biggest problems college students have is time management, which we'll focus on in a later chapter. We over-schedule ourselves or get distracted by other events and end up pushing studying to the very end of the day. This is not ideal. There's no rule that says it has to be dark outside before you start studying. Use the full day to spread your studying out, get more done, and reduce the pressure you put on yourself to cram it all in at night.

- **Study after class.** If you don't have anything else scheduled, studying right after class is the perfect time to do your review then do some work in your other classes as well. Try to leave room in your schedule for this.
- **Study in open blocks of time.** You might have other breaks in your schedule, like between class and a job, or some free hours in the evening before a meeting. Don't put off studying until your entire day is done. Use those one or two hour blocks to knock out some work.
- **Study on a regular basis.** Try to get yourself on a study routine. Things are going to come up that will throw your schedule off, and there will be times when you'll have to concentrate more on one specific course, either for an exam, paper, or project, but don't neglect the others too much.
- **Study in the mornings.** Again, there's no need to give into the college stereotypes of sleeping in 'til noon and staying up until 4 AM for no good reason. You can get a lot done in the mornings. Chances are you'll have more energy and fewer distractions because everyone else will be asleep.
- **Limit the all-nighters.** There's always something going on in life so there are going to be times when you're going to have to be up waaaaay past your bedtime. Whenever you can avoid this situation, please do, because it really can mess with your body cycle. But if you've gotta do it, you've gotta do it. One thing I've found is that my late night sessions were much more productive when I was *doing* something, rather than simply reading something. I could type a paper, work on problems, or discuss things with a group and be able to stay semi-alert. Trying to read a book at 2 AM was a no-win situation for me.

How to study

A lot of students think that the more time you study, the better you'll do. It's true that some courses will require a lot of study time, but if you use poor study techniques, you may end up wasting a lot of time which ultimately makes for an extremely frustrating situation. You'll say to yourself, "I studied for 10 hours straight and I only got a 'C.'" The issue is not how long you studied, but *how* you studied.

- **Me first.** If you're a part of a study group for a particular class, always study by yourself first, before meeting with the group. You don't want to go to the group meeting with nothing to add. Also, you want to work through the material on your own so you know what you don't understand and what you need the group to help you with.
- **Stay active.** Just as when you're in class, your mind needs to stay active when you're studying. Think about what you're doing, don't just go through the motions.
- **Small chunks of time.** Trying to study for 10 hours straight is not a good idea. If you don't drive yourself crazy in the process, you'll start to fatigue and you won't retain as much information. If you're preparing for an exam, you will probably have a large studying time block, but break it up into 1-2 hour pieces, taking 5-10 minute stretch breaks in between. Walk around, go outside, reset yourself. Maybe take a longer break at some point to eat, run errands, or watch a half-hour of TV. Best to multi-task here – eat while you watch TV – to save time!
- **Set targets.** Set a certain amount of pages to read or a number of problems to get done within a specific time span. Don't just sit down and say "I'm about to study," with no clue about what you're trying to get done. If you know what you need to do in a study time block, or over the course of a day of study sessions, you can check yourself to make sure that it gets done.
- **Reward yourself.** After you finish your problem set, watch some TV or go to the gym. After the big midterm, go to see that movie that just came out. Motivate by telling yourself that you can go to dinner after you read 10 more pages. This gives you something to work for and helps you maintain forward progression. But be careful of counter-productivity by saying, "let me hurry up and finish this math nonsense so I can go out," then put forth a rushed, sloppy effort.

What went wrong?

We all start out with the best intentions when we sit down to do our work. We tell ourselves that in the next 2-4 hours, we're going to have read through the assigned chapters, or finished the homework problems, or reviewed a certain amount of material needed for the upcoming midterm. Meanwhile, after 4 hours, you might only be halfway there. Why?

Meet Study Enemy Number One: **Procrastination**. Procrastination can stretch a 2-hour chore into an entire day of wasted time. Procrastination lives in your TV, your phone, your computer, and your bed. Procrastination can drive, too. If you've got a car on campus, procrastination might take you to the mall, or for a spontaneous day trip. But procrastination is not always about fun and games. Sometimes procrastination will have you clean your room, reorganize your files, or take care of errands that you know can wait until *after* your upcoming exam. The worst thing is that procrastination is friends with your friends. Sometimes you'll all hang out together and have a great time doing things you're not supposed to be doing.

Staying motivated

There are going to be days when you just don't want to study. It's hard to still be in classes when the weather starts getting nicer (which, coincidentally, is final exam period at many schools). Sticking to a rigid study schedule is not easy, but it's part of the job requirements of a college student. Here are a few suggestions to help you when times get rough.

- **Study Buddies.** The way this works is that you find someone who you trust, who's serious about their work, and you study together. The two of you can be in different classes, or even different years in school. You meet up, sit at a table, and each do your own work. If you want, you can even tell each other your study goals for your session, and at the end, check to make sure that each of you met your mark. The Study Buddy concept works because you have someone checking you so that you don't fall asleep or procrastinate. Sometimes students taking the same course will pair up, but instead of meeting as a study group and discussing the class, they simply work individually and monitor each other. The pitfall of having a Study Buddy is when friends try to study together and end up socializing. Study Buddies is a business move, not a time to catch up on gossip. You can do that after you're done studying.

- **Peer support.** For many African American youth, there's a culture of downplaying academic success. Intelligence may be equated with "acting white."[1] This is a critical issue which educators must tackle so that more youth take school seriously and can go on to college. Once you're in college, you typically don't have to face this challenge. In fact, there is vast potential for the exact opposite to take place – for peers to nurture, support, and even challenge each other to achieve excellence. Create a support network with your friends, roommates, organization members, and other peer groups. If we all remain interested in and supportive of each other's well-being, even on the simple level of encouraging each other to study hard, the positive effects become contagious and people will set higher expectations for themselves.

- **Balance.** The reason why it's important to use sound study strategies is that if you can stick to the schedule and minimize procrastination, you should have ample time to enjoy yourself outside of your classroom duties. Studying becomes tedious and frustrating when you do it all the time. If you study smart, you won't have to spend every moment in the books, and when it is time to study, you'll have a much more positive attitude. Tell yourself, "if I start this paper early, my whole weekend will be freed up," and see if you don't get energized to make that happen.

- **You've come this far.** This was a great motivator for me at the end of a semester. When you think about the 12 or so weeks you put into a class, all the notes, all the hours of studying, you want to make that mean something. You don't want to go through all of that and end up with a "C" to show for it.

- **Graduation.** Each exam, each paper, each class is another step towards that goal. Keep that in mind and continue pushing forward.

The Bottom Line: Know Thyself

When we were in college, I would drag my girlfriend to the library occasionally. We usually didn't stay that long. Eventually we stopped studying there all together. We just weren't library people.

Some folks can't study in the mornings because they're not fully functional until noon. Others, like me, prefer to get up at 7:00 AM, take care of business, and have the afternoon and evening off. For some people, if the TV's on in the background, it's okay. Others will get sucked right into the show's plot and forget they're trying to get their reading done.

Really, it doesn't matter where you study, when you study, or how long you study. As long as you're using sound techniques and achieving your study goals, continue doing what you're doing. If you find that you're not achieving the results that you should be, be serious about figuring out what's wrong and then make adjustments. Sticking to the same bad formula isn't going to do you any good.

Since her return to school, my former girlfriend, now my wife, studies in the bed, in her PJs, tucked under the covers. She's pulling straight "A's." She's focused, she sets clear goals for her study sessions, and she sticks to them. She knows when she's getting tired and needs to shift locations or take a quick break. That's really what it's all about. You've got to know what works for you and what doesn't, then do the things that work.

>> Step 5: Get Help

This last step is probably the most important, and also the most challenging for African American students, myself included. Even though I was told about the need to get tutors and use my resources in numerous orientations, and by upperclassmen, advisors, and peer mentors, I still carried a chip on my shoulder early on and wanted to "go for self." I didn't want to "waste my time" going to office hours or waiting around for professors after class. I thought I was too smart to need help, but let me tell you, once I realized the deal, I changed my tune quickly. So allow me to introduce you to Brian Peterson's Number One Rule when it comes to asking for help: *Get over your hang ups and get what you need*.

You might be shy. Get over it. You might have scheduling conflicts that make office hours hard to get to. Work it out, or ask the professor to meet you at some other time. You might not want to go through any extra hassles, or spend additional time with a tutor, talking to your professor, or in a review session. Get real – this is college, and that's a part of the program. You might think that getting a tutor is for dummies. Let that thought go immediately. The only dummy is the one who doesn't take advantage of every possible resource he or she can.

In all seriousness, it's very true that African American students may be hesitant to ask for help. You may be distrustful of people you don't know or may fear that people will think you're not as smart. You might feel uncomfortable or not know how to initiate a conversation with a professor. These are all relevant issues, but you must understand that **no one expects you to get through college by yourself**. They provide tutoring and office hours for a reason. Academic resources are definitely not a sign of weakness, but one of strength. Students who use tutoring when they need it get better grades. It's that simple.

If you really feel apprehensive about getting help, bring a friend with you. I was fortunate to have a few buddies in the same major as I was, so we all ended up taking at least one or two of the same classes each term. We all typically went to office hours together, and prepared for exams together, and signed up for a group tutor. In classes where I was by myself, I knew that I had to step up and get whatever help I needed, but soon, it wasn't even an issue. Getting a tutor and using the available help resources on campus eventually came as naturally as signing up for courses, buying books, and going to class. And honestly, that's how you should look at it. It's an essential part of the process.

How can I be down?

Every school will provide a variety of services and resources for students, so you'll want to ask around to see what's available and where to find it. There are also some things you can initiate on your own. Here's a breakdown of what's what, and some tips on using them effectively:

Tutoring. Many schools have a Tutoring Center or an Academic Resource Center which will be your starting point. Many of these departments receive funding which will allow you to have a certain number of free tutoring hours. You may also have a scholarship or fellowship, or be a part of a special program on campus which will provide you with free or low-cost tutoring. Look into your options and see what's available.

- **When to get a tutor?** You probably won't need a tutor for every course. Some schools may limit the amount of tutoring you can sign up for, so choose wisely. If you're taking a difficult course, especially courses in your major, the continuation of a course you had problems with last semester, or one of those classes that everyone says "Wow, you're taking *that*!" getting a tutor is probably a good idea. Sign up for tutoring as early in the semester as possible. Sometimes there's a short supply of tutors, so you want to make sure to get one, plus you want to start off the semester right and work tutoring sessions into your weekly schedule. Don't wait until after you've failed the first midterm. Remember – be *proactive*, not reactive.

- **How to get the most out of a tutor?** You have to come prepared, which means that you need to look at the material before your tutoring session. Having a tutor isn't like a waving a magic wand and all of a sudden understanding. You need to study first, try the problems, then put together your list of questions. And when you meet with them, treat it just like a class – come on time, prepared, alert, and ready to learn. Ideally, you should meet with your tutor once a week, however, some people just need to make appointments occasionally, such as when they're preparing for an exam. See what works best for you.

- **What if your tutor isn't working out?** Not every tutor is going to be great. Some may not have as strong a grasp on the material as they should, or you may have problems scheduling times to meet with them, or you simply may not get along. If this is the case, look into getting another tutor.

- **What if a tutor isn't available?** This can be a challenge, but sometimes you have to draft a tutor. If you need a tutor for a specific chemistry class but none are available, visit the Chemistry Department and ask around. Ask your professor if he knows of any graduate students or former students who might be able to help you. Find out about any chemistry or engineering organizations on campus and see if they can help. If all of that fails, you'll have to make effective use of office hours with the professor and/or TA. I had a couple of courses where no tutor was available, but the TA essentially became my tutor because I was in his office twice a week.

- **Become a tutor.** Here's something you may have never thought about, but when you look at it, it's really a great idea. If you want to go to med school, you'll have to remember the stuff you learned in your intro science courses. If you want to be fluent in Spanish, you'll need to practice it often. One of the best ways to maintain these skills is to teach them. To become a tutor, you need to earn a high grade in the course and be able to demonstrate your knowledge, so right there is incentive to do well in your intro courses. Need more incentive? Tutors get paid well, especially if they know how to hustle. I did group tutoring in calculus, which I ran like a mini-class, averaging about five students at a time, each paying $10/hour. That's $50 for an hour of work. Beyond the cash, it was also a great feeling knowing I was helping these students to really understand the material. So that's just one more positive experience to balance out the times when I may have had a stressful midterm of my own. Plus, tutoring looks good on your résumé because it shows a command of particular subjects and people skills.

Office Hours. Professors and teaching assistants (TAs) have time slots each week where you can visit their offices and ask questions. Office hours serve two purposes. First, it's another opportunity to get help. Secondly, you want to make a connection with the professor and teaching assistant outside of class, especially for courses in your major or of special interest to you. Some people might see this as "brown-nosing" or "kissing up," but it's really all in how you look at it and how you go about it. If you're genuinely interested in the subject and want to know more about the professor's research, a concept they discussed in class, or how you can get better connected to the field, then reaching out to the professor makes perfect sense. If you go to office hours without any specific questions, but think that just because you showed up, the professor will like you and give you a good grade, then you need to revamp your approach.

Prepare for office hours just like you prepare for a tutoring session – spend some time with the material in advance and form specific questions. Properly preparing also means that you shouldn't wait until the very last minute to reach out to the professor, or try to contact them at an unprofessional hour. Don't be afraid to connect with them, but also use common sense. After you've gone the first time, repeat visits become much easier, and overall, using office hours wisely will be a huge benefit for you.

Some things to ask:
- How should you best study for this course?
- How should you best prepare for an upcoming exam?

- How should you best start a research project or paper? What are some good sources to use? Is your topic clear enough?
- How can you do better on the next exam, based on your sketchy initial performance? Discuss your previous study process and get their feedback.
- What's the professor's area of specialty or current research? Has he or she written any articles or books?
- Get advice on additional courses in the department, other professors to connect with, opportunities in the field (research, independent studies, internships).

Study Groups. Used correctly, study groups can be an excellent motivator and a great opportunity to exchange information with classmates. Study groups can meet regularly or just to prepare for an exam. You want to be sure to meet in a location that has the resources you need – the ability to talk without disturbing others, access to a computer if you need it, a board, a table with enough room for everyone, etc.

- **Group membership.** Don't confuse "study groups" with "friends." This is business. You may be fortunate to have some friends in some of your same courses, so it may make sense to form a group. If you do go in with friends, you need to understand that study group time is study group time, not socializing time. Don't limit yourself if you don't know anyone in the course, however. And certainly don't limit your study groups by race. If there aren't any other Black students in class, that doesn't mean that you won't have a group. Seek out students who seem serious about the course and invite them to form a group with you. A group could be as few as you and another person but probably should be no larger than five students. More than that makes it harder to really establish a good system.
- **Setting up the group.** You may want to designate a group leader who will organize the group, split up the work in a way that makes sense, and keep things running smoothly. Or you may want to decide on things by committee.
- **Making it work.** How will your study group function? Will you meet on a regular basis or will you simply meet a few times before an exam? Either way, the most important thing is to set expectations for the overall study group and for each meeting. What do you want to achieve and what's going to be your plan

of attack? How you will you assess whether or not it's working? What if certain group members aren't holding up their end? How do you balance things so everyone benefits, and no one is in danger of being left out? How do you maximize the potential of the group – can you find out who's good at what and specialize that in some way? Your group will work in different ways, typically according to the type of class you're taking. For example, in a problem-solving class, each group member may be assigned a few problems to complete before you meet, then explain them to the entire group. Or you may actually meet up and work on the problems together. For a literature class, you may all do the reading individually then meet to discuss the themes. Talk it through, try out different approaches to determine what style fits best.

Exam Review Sessions. Professors and/or TAs may hold a review session, either during class time or as an additional meeting, in order to prepare for an upcoming exam. **Never skip an exam review session**, even if it's at 7 PM and you're going to miss a rehearsal, your favorite TV show, or your intramural volleyball game. Professors often will really narrow down what you need to study, and even go over problems very similar to exam problems. That's the best case scenario, and one well worth the time investment. Worst case, they go over a bunch of stuff you already know. If that's going on, still sit there until the end (because you never know if they might slip in something useful), and use the time to quietly review material on your own.

Weekly Review and Help Sessions. Departments on campus or specific courses may offer weekly review sessions or similar opportunities for students to receive extra help. Again, don't ignore this or pass it off as a waste of time. Check it out and see what's going on. More than likely, the students who aren't there are going to be the ones struggling on the exam.

Online Help. Similar to the weekly reviews described above, some departments may feature some sort of online help options – maybe having students available to answer questions via message board, chat, or e-mail. This is yet another resource to take advantage of, so keep it in mind.

Writing Help. As we'll cover later in the book, you always want to have someone else proofread a paper before you turn it in. At the very least, get a friend or roommate to look it over quickly. Some schools have writing centers where student volunteers will not only proofread your work, but help you get started with an outline. To use this service, however, you can't wait until the night before the paper is due.

The Library Staff. The library can be an intimidating place. If you can't find what you're looking for, don't be afraid to ask someone. You may not even know everything that your school library has to offer, so again, ask someone for a tour (some schools will have library tours as part of orientation), visit the library website for more information, or simply browse around and see what's inside.

Pre-Professional Societies and Academic Organizations. Groups such as the Student National Medial Association, the National Society of Black Engineers, honors societies, or school-specific groups such as a business club or computer science group can also be a huge benefit. You can network with other students in your major, form study groups, conduct your own research projects (which could lead to a business idea, an independent study, a conference presentation, or other possibilities), get access to books, notes, and old exams, and overall, have an important support base to tap into.

Mentors. A mentor can be an upperclassman, a faculty or staff member, or even an alum from the school. Since there are a variety of mentor types, you'll look for different kinds of information from each. Mentor relationships can form almost on their own, or sometimes never materialize beyond you getting a slip of paper with your mentor's name and contact info. Be open to connecting with them, and if you don't hear from them first, reach out to them. They can be a huge resource for getting around the campus, picking classes or a major, getting an internship, or simply having someone to discuss how you feel.

Academic Counseling. You may be trying your hardest to get this college thing down but feel like you're missing something because you grades are still coming up short. Chances are, you need more focused assistance in a specific area. Maybe your time management is off, or you need to work with someone one-on-one to develop better reading comprehension skills, or put together strategies for approaching different types of classes. Many schools have services available where you can sit down with an academic counselor and get help.

Professional Counseling. We'll talk about this more later, but there may be times when you're going through something and you need someone to help you through it. It could be a problem back home, depression over a relationship, insecurities about your academic performance, or some other issue which is preventing you from focusing and feeling good about yourself. Most schools offer counseling services to help students in need. These services are confidential, so no one will know what was discussed, or that you were even there.

Informal Help. Look around. There's help all over the place. The Resident Advisor in your dorm, the upperclassmen down the hall, the senior in your major who's on the track team with you. College is all about communication and networking, so if you have a question, ask somebody. Most people love to talk, and they feel good when they're able to help someone out. Just think about how you feel when people think highly enough of you to ask you for advice. Don't be afraid to reach out to someone when you need to talk.

Summary

The Formula for Success is indeed a formula, or a systematic way of doing things. For it to work, it needs to become a routine, or a part of your daily life. When we talk about Time Management, we'll look at ways that you can prioritize so that the formula is built into your schedule. Next, we'll talk about some specific skills that will help you excel inside the classroom and out.

SEVEN. THE EXTRA MILE: GOING FURTHER, GETTING SMARTER

This chapter covers additional tips to make your academic journey a smooth one. We'll start out with a look at selecting which courses to take.

>> Choosing Classes

Your school may offer hundreds of courses each semester, so where do you begin? Well, if you've chosen your major already, then you'll probably have a good idea of at least one or two courses that you have to take each term in order to fulfill your graduation requirements. However, you may want to look into general courses and broader electives in your freshman year, in case you change majors. Additionally, since many schools want their students to get a well-rounded academic experience, you'll have other requirements in areas such as foreign languages, humanities, and freshman seminars. This makes things a bit easier, especially in your first year, as your schedule will already be partially mapped out.

If you're still deciding on a major, you will have more flexibility in choosing your classes. Maybe you have an idea of what you want to do, so take courses in that area and make sure they fulfill a requirement. If you really have no clue about what field you want to pursue, then it would probably help to talk with someone – an academic advisor, mentor, upperclassman, professor, or peer counselor, to try to get some direction. Also, be sure to read the chapter on choosing a major if this is a big concern for you right now.

Some schools require you to speak with your academic advisor before registering for classes. This is to ensure that you stay on track and don't just sign up haphazardly for classes. (That's one way to end up on campus for five or more years). Even if you aren't required to meet with your academic advisor, it's a good idea to make an appointment with them periodically to go over your plans. Keep in mind, however, not every advisor is going to truly be in tune with your specific situation and provide the best advice. If something sounds funny to you, seek out a second opinion.

Here are some other points to consider when it's time to sign up for courses:

- **Prerequisites.** If it says that you must take Pysch 200 before you sign up for Pysch 300, don't think it's okay to sign up for the 300-level course without having done 200. In most cases, you'll be much better off having been exposed to the material from the earlier course. In some cases, however, you may actually be qualified to take a course without doing the prerequisites, but talk to the professor, your advisor, and any other relevant people before you find yourself stuck in something that's over your head.

- **Placing out.** If you have AP credit, make sure to get all of the logistics squared away regarding which courses you've placed out of. Speak with your academic advisor or the registration office for details. Even if you did place out, if you don't feel completely comfortable with the material, you may want to take the course anyway, especially if you'll be taking a series of courses in the same subject later.

- **Shop around.** Choosing courses can be like shopping for clothes. If it looks bad in the dressing room or doesn't fit right, you're not going to buy it. Check out several classes the first week of school, or if there's a course being taught at different times by different professors, sit in on each lecture and see which teaching style feels best for you. Be sure to keep the Drop/Add dates in mind, however. Don't let them slip by and leave you locked into a class that you really don't want to be in.

- **Use your pre-shopping resources.** Some schools have detailed course descriptions, reviews of courses and professors, and other related information. You can also get old course syllabi from departments, online, or from students who've taken the course before. Ask students for verbal feedback as well – how was the professor, the workload, the readings, etc? How would they rate the course overall? Use all of this information to make an informed decision about which courses to sign up for.

- **Prioritize.** In your shopping around phase, you may stumble upon a great instructor for a course section, but it doesn't quite fit into your schedule. Re-work your schedule if at all possible, because great teaching will lead to a great class experience. If you absolutely can't manipulate your other responsibilities, then go into the courses that you end up taking with the best attitude possible. That will help get you started off right, with a "taking care of business" mindset.

- **Balance.** Your semester is going to be your life for the next several months. Do you want it to be completely filled with all accounting courses? Are you trying to ruin your GPA by taking four or five very difficult classes? Try to keep things manageable and interesting by knocking out one or two requirements or challenging courses, and a few electives or courses of interest to you. Signing up for a fun class per term or per year will give you something to look forward to and ease the stress of your other courses.

- **Don't put them off.** You don't want to go into your senior year having to complete your language requirement. Make sure you're satisfying graduation requirements as you go (and if possible, take care of most or all of them early), then you can enjoy senior year more, and have time to job-hunt, do grad school apps, or catch up on some much-needed rest!

- **Off semesters.** Consider taking difficult courses in their "off" semester (the semester when most people aren't taking that course), if it's offered and if this works into your 4-year course schedule. There may be less pressure and competition, and you may receive more individualized attention.

- **Summer school.** This is another option. The drawbacks – it's summer, which could kill your internship or travel plans, plus it's an added educational expense. Summer courses also tend to move faster, so be aware of that. The benefit is that there are usually a smaller number of students and there's not much going on around campus, so you can focus your full attention on your work.

- **Another university.** You may be able to take some of your courses at another school, whether it be summer or during the school year. See what your school policy is. The benefit of this is a change of pace and scenery, and for summer school, the opportunity to save some money (by taking courses at a cheaper school) or convenience (by taking courses in or near your hometown). Financial aid eligibility for classes taken at another school can get tricky, and may have you paying the full cost out-of-pocket, so speak with your financial aid counselors to get the full picture.

- **Pass/Fail.** Most schools offer this as a grading option for a set number of courses. Pass/Fail is great when you're taking a course outside of your major that you're not really sure about, or some other elective where you just need a credit, not a grade. Make sure to pass the course, though (ie, do some work!)

- **Guaranteed "A."** There's no such thing, so stop looking for it. Upperclassmen will tell you about the easiest courses on campus, but be careful. No matter what, this is still college, so you'll need to apply yourself. If you prepare for an "A," you should get an "A," but if you do nothing, you might be shooting yourself in the foot. Also, courses change content and/or instructors. I signed up for a class that everyone told me was so easy, but when I took it, they added an extra exam and a research paper. My guaranteed "A" became a counterproductive "B+" and required much more work than I had anticipated.

- **What if the course is full?** Go anyway. A student may drop which could open up a spot for you. Or the professor might extend the enrollment and let you in. Talk to the professor and see what the chances are.

- **Don't sleep.** You're in the middle of the Fall term, getting ready for an exam and working on a research paper, when all of a sudden, people start talking about picking classes for the Spring. Most definitely take care of your Fall class responsibilities, but don't push picking courses off too long because you may end up getting locked out of your choices.

Summary

Choose your courses wisely by consulting with your advisor, reading through the course descriptions, asking around, and using the Drop/Add period to sample different classes and instructors. Know and use the various options like Pass/Fail and summer school. Lastly, don't wait until the last minute to enroll in classes.

>> Getting (and Keeping) Your Books

In the old days (read, "when I was in school") getting your books was a no-brainer. You went to the campus bookstore or you asked around to see if another student would loan or sell you their old copy. Now, you have even more options, and here they are:

- **The Campus Bookstore.** This is still a pretty decent choice. You may find a cheaper price elsewhere, but the bookstore is convenient, since it's on campus, and they should have what you need in stock. Many campus stores carry both new and used editions, so you may be able to save a few bucks.
- **Online stores.** The internet has introduced competitive pricing in the textbook business, and many internet retailers have enormous catalogs with virtually any and every book available to order. Two things to remember when buying online, and both have to do with shipping. First, factor in the shipping costs and make sure you're actually saving money. Secondly, order your books early so that you get them by the time classes start.

  Here are some links to a few popular book websites. There are others out there as well. Just do a search for "College Textbooks" or "Used College Textbooks" for more options.

  o **Amazon.com**
  o **BarnesandNoble.com**
  o **Bookbyte.com**
  o **Bunchesofbooks.com (specializes in used college texts)**
  o **Ecampus.com**
  o **Varsitybooks.com**

  This link does a price comparison of books from several vendors:

  o **Directtextbook.com**

- **Other bookstores.** Bookstores off campus, from chains to used stores, may also be able to help with your needs, and may offer competitive prices. If you don't see your book on the shelf, see if they can order it for you.
- **Buy or borrow from a fellow student.** Ask around – friends, upperclassmen, dormmates, organization members, etc. – and see if anyone has what you need. Many schools also have online resources such as message boards and news groups for students to buy and sell old texts.

- **The library.** Who'd ever think to check out a textbook from the library? Apparently, the early bird does. Some students make it their strategy to check course books from the school library before the rest of the class even has the syllabus in their hand. In some cases, libraries have a "Reserve" section for texts being used in the classroom. Reserve books can't be checked out, but must remain in the library for all students' benefit. The major problem with this is that suppose you need to do a reading but someone else is already using the book that you need. Who knows when they'll be done? And what if you really need to use the text for an extended time – say a few days – to prepare for an exam. Relying on the Reserve copy could put you in a bind.

- **Student group bookshelf.** If you belong to a fraternity, sorority, pre-professional organization, or other student group, you may have an archive of old notes and textbooks from upperclassmen and former group members. If you don't have a resource like this, look into starting one. It's pretty simple to do and could be a valuable tool for future students and organization members.

Early and late

Get your books **early**. This way you can get a head start on the reading. If a class such as a literature or African American studies course has a bunch of books required, get them as you use them in the course. Sometimes the course won't have enough time to cover all of the books, so for those listed later in the syllabus, you may want to wait and see. For courses with only one text, however, don't wait until the week before an exam to buy the book!

Whenever possible, make sure you have the **latest** edition of the text (or whichever version the professor is using in the course – most instructors use the most recent editions). Earlier text editions won't have the most up-to-date information, and the page numbers and content won't match up with the class reading assignments, so you'll be thrown off and miss out on what the rest of the class is getting. If you only have direct access to an older edition, take a look at someone's updated copy so that you can compare and see what's different.

Buy or borrow?

In my opinion, you should buy books for classes in your major because you'll probably refer to them for future courses and also when you get into your career. Additionally, if you buy it, you can write in it, which is an excellent study technique. But if your funds are running low this term, you might have to hustle up some loaners. Books outside your major are up to you – some people love to collect books and others don't need another heavy box to ship back home at the end of the school year.

Keep or sell?

Again, you'll probably want to hold onto books for courses in your major or of interest to you. For some students, however, buying and selling books is a business, and the only way they'll have cash for future books. Keep things in perspective though – if you need to write in the book in order to improve your study tactics and your grades, or if you think that a particular book may be useful down the line, figure out some way to make it happen. If you are going to sell you books, however, some of the links listed previously have a book-seller's section. Do a search for additional online vendors. Also check school message boards, websites, and the campus bookstore.

Loan or hoard?

I'm all in favor of helping people out and have been known to pass books along to folks, but there are some books that I'm not letting go of, and some people that are on my "Do not loan to" list. If you know your friends are irresponsible and will either lose or devalue your book, tell them that they need to get their own (maybe spending their money will teach them how to take care of it). If you trust the person with your merchandise, however, and won't need the book this term, then consider loaning it.

Be sure to set up some guidelines to avoid any misunderstandings. Make it clear that it's a loan not a gift, and let them know when you expect to get your book back. Also let them know whether or not they can write in it (and in pencil or pen). Write your name and contact info somewhere in the book and also keep a list of who you've loaned books to, and their contact info. This may all seem petty, but when you spend your money on a book you want to make sure you get it back, and that it's in good condition. I found out the hard way – when I couldn't remember who I had loaned books to – that if I'm running a library, I need to have a book check-out list and a return policy. Probably should have gotten some collateral, too.

Taking care of your books

Keep them on a bookshelf, not on the floor or piled up any old way. If you don't need to refer to the book or do any reading, then don't carry it around. This lessens the chance of it getting damaged, rained on, pages bent, etc., and is also easier on your back (and backpack – I've seen bags get worn down quickly by college book overload). Finally, when you're moving out for the school year, pack your books snuggly in book boxes so they don't shift around in transit.

Summary

Your books are an investment, and also a potentially valuable re-sell item. Get them early, use them wisely, refer to them often, keep the ones you'll need later, and take good care of them.

>> Finding Your Learning Style

We all have preferences – types of music we like, favorite colors and hangouts, hobbies we enjoy, etc. We also have preferences when it comes to **Learning Style**. Identifying your style will help you understand how you best take in information. And knowing this can help you choose courses or instructors, adjust your study techniques and environment, and pinpoint areas that you need to improve.

There are several schools of thought regarding learning style and related themes. They focus on a variety of theories and reference points, such as multiple intelligences, culturally-specific practices, personality indicators, and others. A full discussion on the various models is beyond the scope of this book, however, we will look at some of the basic ideas. I've also included a list of other sources at the end of this section in case you want to seek out more information. The implications of particular learning styles can factor into the many other facets of your life outside of the classroom, so you may be interested in looking further into this topic.

The styles

You may already know that you don't like math and sciences, which is why you've chosen to major in communications. But in your communications courses, are you aware of what best holds your attention? Do you like it when the professor talks you through concepts, or do you prefer more writing on the board or slides? Or maybe your favorite classes are the ones where the students discuss topics for the majority of the time? Do you like group assignments or would you rather work solo? Can you think in a series of logical steps, or does your mind wander around or become more concerned with *how* instead of what?

With these questions above, we've covered some of the more common styles (or intelligences), such as **Visual**, **Verbal**, **Logical**, and **Interpersonal**. There are others, some of which rarely work their way into the classroom (unless the professor gets creative, as some are known to do), such as **Musical**, **Kinesthetic** (bodily movement), **Intrapersonal** (self-awareness of feelings and beliefs) and **Existential** (spiritual).

The African-centered themes introduced in Chapter 3 are also known as the Black Cultural Learning Style. If you refer back to them, you'll see some overlap with the items just mentioned here. For example, Verbal relates to Orality; Interpersonal is similar to Communalism; Intrapersonal connects with Affect, Expressive Individualism, and maintaining a personal or inner Harmony; Verve relates to a variety of experiences such as Visual, Verbal, and Logical; Kinesthetic is Movement; Existential is Spirituality. Thus, embedded within this cultural framework are academic strategies, and coincidentally, when these strategies are incorporated into the classroom or a Black student's overall learning environment, the student often fairs better.

For example, students may desire a harmonious connection between their school work and what happens in "the real world," and if they don't see it, they may become turned off.[1] Research also shows that though orality is a part of the Black Cultural Learning Style, verve may play a larger role in the classroom setting for African American students. Students can benefit more from a variety of experiences, including discussion and seeing things on the board or via slides.[2] Black students may also show a preference for group work which gives them the opportunity to connect with other classmates, but provide their own unique contribution to the effort.[3] These examples are not true across the board, as we all have our own individual preferences and ideal work environments.

What now?

You may have read through the above text, thought about your learning preferences, and taken a stab at figuring out where you sit with all of this. So now, what do you do with it?

First, it's important to understand that these styles don't cancel each other out. You may have said to yourself, "I like when the professor talks *and* shows diagrams," or "Sometimes I want to work in a group, but other times I'd rather work alone." You can be good in more than one of the areas. You can excel in them all, if you're so fortunate. Or some skills may not be up your alley. You may not play a musical instrument, be good at reading a map, or particularly enjoy a completely lecture-based course.

In some cases, you're going to need to identify your weaknesses and shore them up, because unfortunately, many college professors teach a certain way, have been doing it for years, and ain't changing. Boosting your skills in their particular teaching style will help you absorb more information in class. Here are some suggestions for you to explore:

- **Conversion.** If the teacher likes talking, but you like pictures, learn how to transfer their material into concept maps. Take good notes in class, and later when you're reviewing, look for connections and create diagrams or charts which will help the information make more sense to you. You can vary this approach in many ways to fit your style – reading notes out loud, discussing things with study groups, converting diagrams or logical steps into a paragraph or a format that you better relate to.

- **Focus your attention.** You may not enjoy following along on the many slides your professors slows in class, but make sure you focus in on the details and capture the information.
- **Talk it through.** We discussed this in the Study Skills chapter, but when you're in a lecture course, keep a conversation going in your mind about what's going on. Ask questions and think about what's being said.
- **Look for patterns and similarities.** You may not be very comfortable with abstract thinking, but identifying similarities is a good way to get started.
- **Use your senses.** Pay attention to how you feel and how people in your group or class feel. This will help you get more in tune with yourself and relate well with others.

For more information on learning styles, including self-assessment exercises and other tools to help you identify and understand your learning style, visit www.lionsstory.org/college.

>> Beyond the Syllabus

When I was putting this book together, I gathered research from numerous sources on the various topics I wanted to cover. I wanted to look at different view points and examples, sort through a variety of suggestions and advice, and see what was being done at colleges across the country. I explored information on subjects that I didn't even cover in great depth so that I could ensure that my perspective was broad enough and that the content I presented was accurate.

My research process was in itself an empowering learning experience. It was also something that I looked forward to because the subjects interested me. I often found myself losing time clicking through different websites, browsing articles, and going back and forth to the library or bookstore. The information presented here is just a small sample of what I examined. Fortunately, since I'm involved in a number of other educational projects, I was able to apply the data to several areas, which made the time I spent even more worthwhile.

This is how you must approach your academics. It's not about simply fulfilling what's listed on the syllabus, or doing the bare minimum. This is *your* education. You will get out of it what you're willing to put in. Develop a passion for your coursework, especially your major. Go above and beyond expectations. Read related books not listed on the syllabus, look up articles online, and seek out other learning and networking opportunities. In our age of the internet, the amount of information you have at your fingertips is unparalleled, so take advantage of it and create continuing opportunities to learn and grow.

EIGHT. FOUR ESSENTIAL SKILLS

This chapter is going to discuss techniques and strategies you can use in four critical academic exercises: **Reading Comprehension**, **Writing Papers**, **Problem-Solving** (i.e., math, science, statistics, etc.), and **Class Presentations**. These skills often overlap. For example, you may have a chemistry exam with problems and a few essay questions, or your sociology course may require a presentation, a research paper, readings, *and* problem sets, so read through each section carefully and think about how you can work these methods into your academic toolset.

>> Reading Comprehension

> com·pre·hen·sion
> **1 a** : the act or action of grasping with the intellect : **UNDERSTANDING.**[1]

Have you ever read something, then right afterwards said "Huh?" because you had absolutely no idea what was going on? If you've opened up a college textbook before, then I'm sure you know what I'm talking about.

Regardless of your major, you're going to do a lot of reading, so you need to be able to make sense out of what's on the pages. Ultimately, you need to be able to **understand** what you've read, **retain** at least the main concepts in your memory, and be able to **apply** the information according to the course requirements.

The reading assigned to you in college may be lengthy and deal with complex and unfamiliar topics. It's often not the most exciting stuff in the world, either. It's even more difficult for many students to get through the material because they simply do not have good reading techniques. Again, it's unfair to place the blame on students because many of you were never exposed to different reading strategies. For that reason, we see some of the following **common reading problems in college**:

- **Sequential Reading.** Many students start on the first page of the assignment and work through to the end because this is the only way they've ever read. A textbook is not a novel or a who-done-it mystery. It's perfectly fine to read the summary first. You actually want to do this – we'll talk about this more in a second. Another form of sequential reading is reading through a 20 or 30 page chunk non-stop. Instead of reading straight through, you want to look at just a few pages, pause and reflect, take notes or jot down a question, then continue to the next few pages. Again, we'll go into more detail about this later in the chapter.

- **Word for word.** You don't have to read every word on the page. Worse, you don't have to say the word in your head.

- **Looking at the pages.** Just as there's a difference between *listening* and *hearing*, there's also a difference between *reading* and *looking*. Just because your eyes see the words doesn't mean that you're actually reading them. If you read something but can't remember what it was, then you weren't really reading.

- **One and done.** This used to be my personal philosophy, because I didn't enjoy reading. I was only reading something one time, regardless of how much I understood. Those low grades my sophomore year when my courses got a little harder are a direct result of this lazy logic.

- **Skip it.** This was also a product of laziness, but if I was reading and came across a word I didn't recognize, I often wouldn't bother to look it up. Doesn't really do a lot of good to read words that you don't understand.

- **Self-taught speed-reading.** It's not a race. While you do want to get through your assignments efficiently, you also want to make sure that you're getting something out of them. Students who try to breeze through a reading assignment using a homespun speed-reading technique, like reading the first word of every line, or reading the first page and the last, may as well keep the book shut and do something else.

- **Too many pages.** This is more of a time management issue, but when students wait until the last minute and are forced to read a few hundred pages in one sitting, they're setting themselves up for tired eyes and a poor grade.

Reading is studying!

Let me repeat that, so I know that you heard me. *Reading is studying*. When you're reading a textbook, or even a novel for a college literature course, you need to be studying and processing the information. You need to know what you're reading, what you're looking for, and how it will be used. When you sit down to do your reading, you need to approach it as a studying and information gathering session. Your reading techniques must support this objective. Your environment must be supportive as well, so refer to the suggestions we discussed in Chapter 6 to minimize distractions and make the most of your time.

Look before your read

When you first get your textbook, spend a little bit of quality time with it, before you get into the first reading assignment. This will give you an overall feel of what you'll be getting from the book over the course of the semester. Look through the table of contents to see how it's broken down. Compare this to the course syllabus and assess exactly how much of the book you'll be reading. Will you go in chapter order or will you be skipping around? What about the chapters that you're not covering – is there anything interesting in there that you may want to read for yourself at some point, or something that you can use for another course?

Look for information about the author and other contributors – read the introduction, the preface, the acknowledgements, and the "About the Author" page. What has this author done in the field of study? Do they teach anywhere? Do they have other books?

Thumb through the book and see how the chapters are laid out. Look for useful section headers and summary pages spread through the text. Check for questions and problem sets (and an answer key in the back, possibly). Also see if the text has a lot of pictures, sidebars of information, charts, tables, graphs, or other similar items. This will help you gauge how fast your reading will go by identifying points that aren't actual text.

Understand your purpose

Think about why each reading assignment has been given (and no, the answer is not to torture you). What does the professor want you to take from it? What should you be looking for? How can you use the information?

Answering these questions and understanding the purpose of the reading will help you focus your reading sessions and gauge whether or not the reading has been worthwhile. If you have an idea of what you're looking for in advance, you'll know if you've found it.

Reading to Learn

The following approach is a modification of popular SQ3R method (Survey, Question, Read, Recite, Review). It goes above and beyond simply opening up the book and diving in, so it may take some getting used to. Also, with its several steps, it may seem like a lot of work. You will have to put a little extra effort in, but none of the steps are complex or require that much additional time, and what extra time you do spend will benefit you in the long run. After you practice this method a few times, you'll understand the advantages.

Step One: Preview the reading assignment (Survey/Skim, and Form Questions)

Before you actually do the reading, take a few minutes to look through it and think about what you see. Many of you already do this for about 30 seconds when you think about how many pages the assignment is, then thumb through it to check for pictures or other things you won't need to read. Do that, then skim the introduction or the first few paragraphs. Flip through the pages and look at the various section headings, charts, pictures, etc. Once you get to the end of the assignment, read the summary, and look at any end of chapter questions.

Think about those questions in relation to the chapter headings you read. Now think about everything you've previewed and ask yourself the following: What was familiar? What looked confusing? What do you need to know? How does this relate to what's going on in class? These questions will help focus your reading as you go.

Finally, estimate how long it's going to take for you to do the reading, then map out your time management plan – read some sections now, some later, or read it all at once if it's not too lengthy.

Step Two: Actively read and take notes.

Now you will read the assignment, taking whatever time is necessary to finish the job. If you're breaking the assignment up, set a target point to reach then pause and resume later.

The way that you read will depend on your personal preference and also the type of material. Some people can read larger chunks then pause for notes and reflection, while others like to make notes as they go. If the subject is unfamiliar, be prepared to take more notes, if this is your technique. Here are some more tips to guide your work:

- **Answer your questions.** As you go, think about the questions from the end of the chapter or the ones you created in Step 1. Jot down answers in your notebook. You may develop new questions while reading, so write them down and look for answers within the text, or seek help at your next opportunity.

- **Take notes.** In your notebook, write down any vocabulary words, ideas, definitions, or themes that you'll need later. Label the page "Reading Notes" and write down the chapter(s) and page numbers you're reading. This will help keep your notes organized and make things easier to find.

- **Notate the book.** You can also jot paragraph summaries in the margin of your book. This requires just a few words or a phrase to explain what a paragraph or section was about. This will help you quickly recall the information. Underline key words or ideas in the text as well, so that your eyes will quickly focus in on them when reviewing. Some students will prefer to make notes in their book in lieu of taking separate notes, while others may do both, or just take separate notes. See what works best for you. Different approaches may work better for some courses than others. One final word of caution – do not underline large areas of your book. This is time consuming and defeats the purpose.

- **Take small bites.** This technique is especially good for those of us with small attention spans. Read a few pages (1-3), then pause for a minute and think about what you've just read.

Give a quick summary out loud or in your head, or use this pause to take your written notes. Another benefit of this method is that it makes re-reading more tolerable. Instead of having to go back through the whole passage, you'll just need to read the small sections that didn't quite sink in the first time.

- **Keep a dictionary handy.** You'll need this for unfamiliar terms.

Step Three: Summarize (Immediate Review)

After you've completed the entire reading assignment, do a quick summary. This is especially important if you had a lot of pages to go through, and/or spread it out over a few days. Do a summary after each day's work, and on the final day, review the entire assignment.

A simple review would consist of looking at your notes and seeing how much you can recall from the text. Do the summaries in the book margin remind you of what you read? Do your notes capture the main ideas in enough detail? Do you have a good grasp of the information?

A more in depth review method is to write a summary of the reading assignment. Write it as if you are trying to explain the reading to a classmate. In your own words, summarize the main ideas and themes, pulling from the notes you took on paper or in the book. You can also take your written summary further, exploring connections to the class, critiquing the author's views, or giving your personal feedback on the reading.

Step Four: Review (Later Review)

Many of us can't remember what we had for breakfast yesterday, so you're probably not going to remember much of what you read three days ago. Look through your notes periodically to refresh your memory. This way, when the exam rolls around, you would have worked with the information a few times already.

Before reading a new assignment, look through your textbook markings and/or notes from the previous reading as a warm-up. If you summarized sections well in the margins and/or took concise notes, your review should only take a few minutes, but be a valuable learning session and keep you caught up with the course material.

Additional notes and questions

- **What if you don't like reading?** Learn to like it – the sooner the better. Going into it with a bad attitude isn't going to help. The best way to appreciate reading is to read something that you might enjoy. Carve out some time to read a magazine, some fiction, a "how-to" book about a subject of interest, or even info on a favorite website. Carry something around to read during downtimes – transit, standing in line, etc.

- **What if you think you read too slowly?** Comprehension is much more important than speed, however, being an efficient reader can help in your overall time management program. Some quick tips to improve your reading rate are to make sure you're concentrating while you're reading (distractions can considerably stretch out the process or cause you to have to read things multiple times), avoid sounding words out either in your head or whispering them (your eyes move faster than your mouth), and focus your eyes on 3 or 4 words per line, instead of looking at each word individually. For more information on reading rates, check out www.lionsstory.org/college.

- **Break it up.** Start your reading assignments earlier so that you aren't forced to go through them all in one night. Spread long assignments out over a couple of days, or read a block of pages, take a short break, then return.

- **Read earlier.** Whenever possible, don't wait until the end of the day to start reading. Try the mornings or afternoons.

- **Good lighting.** Don't unnecessarily strain your eyes or put yourself to sleep.

- **Compare notes.** If you're unsure about your techniques, check out a classmate's book to see what kinds of notes they've written in their margins, or underlines they've made. If they've taken notes on the readings, ask to view those as well.

- **What if all of this still isn't helping?** If you feel like you're having trouble comprehending what you're reading, seek an academic counselor. They can diagnose your situation and offer more in-depth direction. You may also be experiencing vision problems, in which case you should visit the eye doctor.

Summary

Much like listening in class, you need to keep your mind active when you read and seek out the specific information that you'll need. Be as refreshed as possible when reading – have a good attitude and try not to put off reading until late at night. Most of all, treat reading as a study session, and learn to appreciate reading by doing it as often as you can, both for school and for pleasure.

>> Writing Papers

You may be an economics major or studying physics, an education student or an engineer – it really doesn't matter. You're going to be doing some writing.

People think of writing papers as an intense exercise. Sometimes it can be, like when you're working on your thesis or dissertation. But the same skills used to churn out 20 pages or more are also needed for a one or two-paragraph mini-essay. There are many forms of writing: research papers, reflections, journals, essays, narratives, short-stories, biographies, poetry, articles, lab reports, and more. Each format has its own style, layout, and content requirements, but all depend on your ability to clearly communicate and support your ideas via written words.

The suggestions I'll cover are based on writing assignments involving research, however, you'll be able to apply aspects of the techniques to other writing formats. The advice is broken down into the following sections: **The Planning and Research Stage**, **The Writing Stage**, and **Before You Hand it In**.

Planning and research

In order to take full advantage of this stage – and the entire writing process – you'll need to accurately gauge the scope of the project and give yourself enough time to complete the task.

- **What to write about?** For some writing assignments, such as an essay in response to a given question, reading assignment, or theme, you won't have a choice in the matter.

For papers where you're able to choose a topic yourself, the most important things are to **choose something that interests you** (so that you'll be more excited about doing the paper) and **make sure that the topic satisfies the assignment requirements**. In other words, pick something that you'll be able to find enough information on, and that will generate a good paper. Ask yourself whether the topic is too broad or too narrow, then reevaluate. Also think of a backup topic or two in case your first option doesn't work out.

- **Build on previous work.** Suppose you're a sociology major. There's no rule that says you can't use a paper from Sociology 101 as a starting point for a paper due in Sociology 310. Hold onto your old work so that you can pull things from it down the line. In the interest of education, however, don't always choose the same topic. The point of a paper is for you to explore ideas and learn something, so expose yourself to different areas and themes.

- **Understand the expectations.** If your writing assignment is a comparison study, make sure to do a comparison. If you're doing a research paper, make sure that you've looked up information. I've had students who clearly waited until last minute and turned in research papers based mostly on personal opinions. If you don't follow the directions, you won't earn a good score. Think about the *type* of paper you're supposed to do, and plan your approach accordingly.

- **Talk to the professor.** It's always a good idea to run your topic choice by the class instructor, especially if you're not sure if it's clear enough, or will be a suitable choice. They can help you focus the idea and may provide you with a list of resources to get your research started.

- **Read.** If you're not familiar with academic writing, read academic articles (ask your professor or librarian for some examples). Reading in general – magazines, websites, books, etc. – will help you with sentence structure, writing techniques, vocabulary, and more.

- **Free write.** This is often an effective way to jumpstart the project. Before you start researching or actually writing the paper, type or write out whatever comes to mind – what do you already know, what do you want to do with your paper, what do you need to find out, what are some sources you can use.

- **Do your research.** Don't underestimate the time that it will take you to research your topic. Look at a variety of sources such as books, articles, websites, or audio/video. You can also conduct interviews or surveys, if appropriate. Make sure your sources are as current as possible and that the ideas expressed are still relevant and accepted in academia. Also be aware of the different research sources and options you have. The library obviously has books, but may also have access to online journals, videos, databases, and much more. Ask around. Also, don't rely on the same websites all the time. Do an extensive search so that you can be exposed to as much information as possible. Bookmark good websites for future use.

- **Take useful notes.** Make sure your research counts. If you're pulling out quotations and excerpts from sources to use as supporting arguments, copy them verbatim and list the page number and publication information of the source. If you're gathering background information, write out the ideas neatly and clearly, in a way that makes sense to you. Some people use notecards with a subject heading at the top. Some jot down or type their notes. If you're pulling stuff from the internet, you can simply cut and paste it. If it's coming from a book or other print source, make photocopies when needed.
- **Use the Writing Center.** Many schools have a writing center or some type of similar resource that will help students step through a paper. They can assist with narrowing down your topic, how and where to do the research, how to arrange your ideas, and how to turn out an effective product. If you have trouble writing, or even if you think you're pretty good, check out this resource and see what they have to offer.
- **Start early.** Think about the context of the paper, the number of pages required, and your own comfort level with writing assignments. Estimate how much time you think you'll need, then make sure that you create that time. If you wait until the last minute you'll be cutting yourself off from valuable resources that would have benefited you.

Writing the paper

The key to this stage is developing your own approach and method for constructing your papers. Once you reach a certain comfort level, you'll have your own routine down and welcome the challenge of writing assignments.

The items below discuss different options and tricks that you can use. By doing a thorough job in the Planning and Research phase, the writing process will be much easier to get through.

- **Follow the guidelines.** The professor will establish a format for the assignment (page count, title page, spacing, etc.). Keep this in mind as you work – some people like to start out in the correct format and others will adjust the look of their paper at the very end, but either way, make sure that it meets the requirements before you turn it in.

- **Get organized.** Create a clear, well-written paper by organizing your thoughts. Sort through the notes and ideas you've gathered. Create an outline or a diagram of the different sections of your paper. Now see where all of your material fits in. You can cut and paste things in a computer file, arrange note cards, or use some other method. This will help you understand what you're working with.

- **Write with purpose and style.** Again, keeping in mind the format of your assignment, make sure your sentences and paragraphs help your paper, not hurt it. Your paper can't simply be a bunch of other people's quotes or research scotch-taped together. You need to insert your own thoughts and personality. Think about how other people would critique your work to help you assess its clarity. As you develop as a writer, you'll have different styles or voices you can incorporate, almost like a role-play. I have an "academic" style of writing, a more informal tone I use for fiction, a comedic style, etc. Control the tone of your work by becoming more comfortable with your own techniques. Also, don't be afraid to be creative, within the guidelines and expectations of the assignment.

- **Be clear and fluid.** Most of us don't think linearly, meaning that we may be writing the conclusion of the paper, but suddenly come up with something good to add back to the body. Some people, unfortunately, type the way they think, so within one paragraph are a series of unrelated statements. When you type up your paper in one sitting the night before it's due, you risk producing an erratic piece of nonsense. You'll read it (after the professor has given you a "D") and not be able to make sense of it yourself. Your thoughts must be clear and follow an order. Your introduction must lead to the body of your paper, which must lead to the conclusion. Within each paragraph, your sentences should flow together seamlessly. Again, read good writing so you can get a feel for how it should be done.

- **Make your words work for you.** Use words **efficiently**. If you can say something more clearly with fewer words then trim the fat. Use words **effectively**. Think of strong words that invoke feeling and prove your points. **Vary** your word choices. If you find yourself repeating the same words all the time, consult a thesaurus for other options. But be careful not to **abuse** words. You want to sound intelligent, but don't overdo it with the SAT vocabulary words. Words should be used **correctly**. Watch for things like *capitol/capital*, and *there/they're/their*. If you're unclear on the meaning of a word, look it up before you plop it in your paper.

- **See the professor again.** Some professors will critique a draft to at least let you know if you're headed in the right direction. Better to run questions by them while you're in-progress than to wait until you've finished and be told that you had room for improvement.

- **Improve upon perfection.** Some students do a rough draft or outline in pen and a final version on computer. Others do a series of drafts, all on their laptop. Whatever you do, don't type a paper in one sitting and turn it in, because that's essentially just a draft. You may think it's great, but when you read through it again, you'll realize that it's not. Step back through your papers – each time is an opportunity to make a point clearer, cut out unnecessary words, fix an awkward phrase, or improve the paper in some other way.

- **Switch gears.** If you get stuck while writing, put it on pause and study for another subject. I often find it helpful to come back to something in a few hours, or even the next morning. This is why it's important to give yourself time to work on your papers, rather than wait until the night before it's due.

- **Cite as you go.** This is another effective strategy that will save you time. Plug in your citations or footnotes as you work on the paper, instead of doing it all at the end. You can do the same thing with your "Works Cited" page. Check with your instructor for the citation method that they want to use, or use one of the standard formats, such as MLA or Chicago (Note: use only one format in your paper). For a look at how to setup your citations, visit www.lionsstory.org/college.

- **Number the pages.** It looks good and will help you refer back to things later. Don't write the numbers in, though. Make sure they are printed when you print your final draft.

- **Between the margins.** You need 10 pages. You have 9. Don't count the title page as your 10th and call it a day. The first trick you can do is to subtly adjust the margins. The operative term is *subtle*. The largest side margin you should ever use is 1.25 inches. The smallest is 0.75. Typically you work with 1 inch (although Microsoft Word defaults to 1.25). You can also play with the top and bottom margins, going anywhere from 0.8 to 1.2 inches (default is 1 inch). Some professors may specify a margin size they want you to use, and if they do, don't deviate. Move on to the fonts, but...

- **Stick with the basics.** Do not turn in a paper typed in a `ridiculously huge font` (Courier New, 12-point), or a *script like this* (Monotype Corsiva, 11-point). Use something simple and standard like Arial, Times New Roman, or a similar, easy-to-read style. Also stay with a 10, 11, or 12-point font size. At the same size, Arial takes up more space than Times New Roman. Bookman Old Style, which looks similar to Times, takes up even more space than Arial. Play around with others, but like I said, don't blow it with an ugly 14-point font, and never turn in a paper with all of the text in **bold**.

- **Spacing.** Most papers should be double-spaced. Your professor will let you know, but if they don't, ask. If you have too much material, you can usually get away with using one-and-half line spacing, instead of double. The only time you'll single-space is when it's specified to do so.

- **Don't plagiarize.** Professors have been fired and students have been expelled for lifting other people's work. It's perfectly fine to pull a quote from a book, or some text that supports your point, as long as you cite the source. Don't copy passages from a book (or other source) and call it your own.

- **Back it up.** As you type, maintain a backup copy of your paper on disk, rewriteable CD, or e-mail it to yourself as an attachment. If something happens to the original and you don't have a backup, you're back to square one.

Before you turn your paper in

You've done the preparation and research, and you've put together a well-thought out paper, so please, whatever you do, don't get points deducted now for something stupid.

- **Proofread.** Ideally, you should have someone else look at your paper – a friend, classmate, or roommate. If you can't track anyone down, at the very least, read the paper **out loud** to yourself. This slows your reading pace and will help you find typos. Also, instead of proofreading on the computer screen, print it out and proofread on paper. You'll see things that you didn't see before. Misspeeled wurds stand out. Sea what I mean? If you have too many, an instructor will think you didn't take the assignment seriously, even if you really did put your time into the research and writing. If you know you have ongoing grammatical problems, difficulties with sentence structure or spelling, get help with the entire process of writing your paper. Lastly, use the built-in tools in programs such as Microsoft Word, like spelling and grammar check. They make proofing much easier, even as you type, by underlining possible errors and auto-correcting common mistakes.

- **Title page.** The professor may give you a title page format to use. If not, include the following:

Title of Paper, or Topic of Paper
Your Name
The Professor's Name
The Course Name and Number
The Date

This information can be put on a separate title page, about halfway down the page and centered (as shown above), or on the first page of your paper, in the upper left of the page, left-justified. If you put it on the first page, your name should be the top line, and the title of the paper should come two spaces after the date and be centered.

- **Staple it.** Unless the professor gives you some other method for turning in your paper (inside a clear cover, folder, etc.), make sure you staple it. Do not fold over the upper corners in lieu of stapling! You're not in fifth grade any more.

- **Protect the pages.** Don't turn in a paper that got crinkled up in your backpack or has a coffee stain on the cover. Put it inside of a folder in your backpack so it doesn't get bent, then make sure to keep it clean until it's out of your hands.

- **Meet the deadline.** Some professors maintain a strict policy that deducts points from any and all late papers (if they accept it at all). They won't want to hear your sad story. Other instructors are more lenient and may even grant you an extension, but don't play that game. It's just going to make you stretch out the assignment even further and take away from time that you should be spending on something else. Due dates aren't a surprise, so plan out your time and be professional about turning in your work.

Summary: Make the most of it!

Unlike an exam, you have the opportunity to dictate the terms when writing a paper. Motivate yourself to put together the best paper possible, making it your goal to impress the instructor with your thoroughness and solid writing. Content typically outshines correctness, so even if your paper does have a typo or two, if your ideas and writing style show that you put thought and effort in, you should earn a high grade. This "A" is within your reach, so set your sights on it and make it happen.

>> Problem Solving

When you hear the term "Problem Solving" you typically think of a math course, or those problems in physics using the pulley or computing friction on an incline. There are many subject areas and specific courses that are based on calculations, however, and the skills needed for solving problems can be applied to various other areas, such as organizing your thoughts for a paper (logical ordering), planning your day (estimation and ordering), and even putting together furniture from Ikea (understanding diagrams and the ability to follow specific steps). So even if you're not a "math person," read through the following section for some useful tips. And all of my math, science, and engineering people, this one is definitely for you, so pay attention.

- **Create ongoing study groups.** Get with a group of classmates and pick one or two times a week to hook up and go through problems. This is probably the most important step because 1) it keeps you caught up with the material (you should study on your own and try the problems before meeting with the group), 2) it provides built-in peer support, help opportunities, motivation, and review sessions. Don't wait until midterms to organize a group. Do it from day one, go over the first homework together, then you'll all be much better prepared come exam time. And don't make any excuses about getting with a study group. If you're not the only student in the course, there's no reason why you can't form a group.

- **Do every homework assignment.** Even if it's not collected, do it. Don't wait until the night before it's due to start it. Begin sooner so that you can work on it with your group after you've looked at it yourself, then get extra help via tutoring or office hours if necessary.

- **Do even more problems.** Go beyond the homework. If there are more problems in the book, do them. Or look online. Or start doing old exam problems. You can also get topic-based books, such as MCAT prep or a calculus tutorial/reference, which will have plenty of problems. Look for problems related to what you're doing in class and work through them.

- **When you get stuck.** There will be problems that are going to be difficult for you. Spend some time struggling with them, attacking and analyzing from different angles. After a while if you're still not getting any where, put it to the side and seek help as soon as possible via your study group, office hours, tutoring, an e-mail to the professor, etc. Never spend all night on one problem because then you won't have time for anything else. Also seek out regular reviews or extra-help sessions specific to your class.

- **Create a Problem Bank.** Pick a difficult problem from each homework, quiz, or an example gone over in class, that represents one of the concepts or uses one of the formulas you've learned. Keep adding to your bank as the semester progresses and use the problems to review the material and prepare for exams.

- **Concern yourself with the bigger picture.** It's great to plug in pieces of the equation to get the right answer, but do you understand what you just solved? What does this problem mean in the context of the course? Learn to think critically about the problem so that you can understand the what's and how's, and not just the solution.

- **Rework the problem.** Try switching the problem around, using the answer you found to solve for one of the givens. This is often a tactic on exams, so practice manipulating the questions and solving for different items.

- **Draw a picture.** If a concept or question is unclear at first, it may help to draw a diagram, plugging in all the given information, and visualize what's going on.

- **Write it out.** Try explaining the steps you've taken to solve a problem. Write them down or talk them through. This will help you solidify your understanding of the process and also possibly give some broader insight.

- **Learn from your mistakes.** When you get a corrected homework assignment back, or a midterm, step through it and see what you got wrong, then make sure that you know how to get it right next time. Final exam questions sometimes come straight from the midterm or homework. It may benefit you to do the corrected homework or midterm again, as if it were just given to you.

- **Be careful.** Definitely connect with a study group, but don't rely completely on them. Don't come to the group unprepared, and don't think that the purpose of the group is to give you all the answers. To be functional, the group will depend on everyone's input. Groups are a compliment to individual studying, not a substitute.

Summary

Courses based on problem solving can often be a challenge and require additional time, however, when you apply sound strategies, the process becomes easier. They best way to become successful at problem solving is to do as many problems as possible, get help with the difficult ones, then review the steps often so you remember how it's done.

>> Class Presentations

So, you just skimmed through the course syllabus and see that you have to do a presentation in front of the class later in the semester. Rule Numero Uno – **suck it up, get over it, and put on your happy face**. There's no getting around it, so let go of the negative attitude (if you had one – believe it or not, there are some people who actually *like* class presentations). Here are some tips to help you get through it and do the job right, broken down into three stages: **Early Preparation**, **Final Preparation**, and **Presentation Day**.

Early Preparation

- **Do your research**. How are you going to present some shoddy, last minute, thrown together mess? This undoubtedly will blow up in front of the whole class. Make sure to thoroughly research your topic beforehand.
- **Keep it simple**. Most presentations have a time limit. If yours is supposed to be ten minutes, you might think this is a long time, but when you start putting it together, you'll find that it goes by quickly, especially when it's a group presentation. The only time ten minutes seems long is when you have absolutely no idea what you're talking about. If you do your research and plan things out, you won't have that problem. In fact, you'll probably have to scale your presentation down because you won't have time to say everything that you'd like. Pick out the important points and sell them well. Imagine being in the audience of your own presentation, and make sure that what you're saying is clear and makes sense.
- **Be creative.** Try looking at this presentation thing from another angle. Imagine it's a performance. That's not so much of a stretch, since you have an audience. Think about interesting ways to keep their attention, and even entertain them, while effectively getting your message across. Can you include a relevant comic strip as a handout or slide? Can you demonstrate something? Can you act out or role-play part of your presentation (demonstrate the quality customer service that helped a product exceed sales expectations, show the difference between overt and subtle racism).
- **Use Powerpoint wisely**. A fancy, graphically intense Powerpoint slide may look wonderful on your computer screen, but be completely unreadable when projected. Additionally, slides are for bullet points, diagrams, or charts, not for your entire presentation text. Again, the key here is to keep it simple, making sure your slides enhance the presentation instead of take away from it.
- **The network's down**. If you're relying on the internet as part of your presentation, don't. Save a copy of the web page or video you want to display to your laptop's hard drive. I've been to numerous technology conferences where something went wrong trying to show something "live" on the net, and these are computer professionals! Only use the internet in your presentation if you can't find another alternative.

- **Have a backup plan**. It's a good idea to have a hardcopy of your slides, or to know how your presentation will flow without showing that internet video clip, in case the technology isn't acting right on presentation day.

Final Preparation

- **Do a dress rehearsal**. If you're doing a solo presentation, you need to time it beforehand to know how it's going to flow. If you've got a group presentation, you have to work out each person's part to make sure it all fits smoothly. Treat your rehearsal as the real deal – go through your slides and say your part. This will give the group a final opportunity to critique each other. Pretend you have an audience or practice in front of some friends. *Never do your presentation for the first time during class.*
- **Stick to the time limit**. Professors put a time limit on the presentations for a reason. Part of the challenge is to work with this restriction. Going under time will show that you didn't find enough material. Going overtime isn't cool either, because it pushes everything off schedule. Get as close to the time limit as possible. Also, find out beforehand whether there's a Question and Answer (Q&A) portion, and if this is included in your time limit or separate.
- **Anticipate questions.** Most presentations allow for a Q&A portion at the end. Think about what might be asked of you then map out some possible answers.

Presentation Day

- **Business attire required**. You'll be tempted to wear your usual jeans and t-shirt, but please do better than that. You don't have to pull out your prom outfit, but stepping up your gear on presentation day shows that you're taking it seriously. As a general rule, treat all presentations like job interviews, and dress accordingly.
- **Arrive early**. Test your slides or other tech gadgets. Make sure you have everything you need, then sit back and get ready for your turn.
- **Breathe easy (and smile).** I used to get butterflies every time I thought about having to stand up in front of a room of people,

but now, I've done it so much that it doesn't phase me any more. Sometimes I even look forward to it. I look at presentations as a conversation. It's really no different than sitting down and talking to one person. Yeah, all eyes may be on you, but what's the problem with that? Why does this make us nervous? We think we're going to mess up or say something stupid, and sometimes we will, but that's okay. You'll correct yourself then move on. Don't put extra pressure on yourself because you'll only tense up and not be able to focus. Relax, use note cards or an outline sheet if you think you're going to forget something, and just be yourself, talking to a friend. Before you start, introduce yourself and your presentation topic, then keep your head up to maintain eye contact and project your voice so everyone can hear you. Glance at your notes when you need to, but don't read from them the whole time. Speak at a comfortable pace; don't rush through it. Also avoid saying "um," "uh," and "you know what I'm saying." If you were nervous at the start, one or two minutes in, you won't even remember. And if you've prepared and done a practice run, you have absolutely nothing to worry about.

Summary

Course presentations aren't nearly as hard as we initially make them out to be. The professor does it every day. And in a discussion course, you're already voicing your opinions, so don't be afraid of doing the same thing in front of the classroom. Do your research, plan what you want to say, and practice it beforehand, preferably in front of an audience or in the mirror. Your rehearsals will make you more comfortable and confident when it's time for the real thing.

We've covered studying, reading, and writing skills, and now we've arrived at the moment that probably puts the most fear in college students' hearts – exam time.

Whether it's a midterm or a final, exams typically make us nervous for a number of reasons. For starters, they're hard. If they weren't, it wouldn't be college. There's also a lot riding on them. For a course that gives one midterm and a final exam, that's only two chances to earn your grade. That's a lot of pressure.

Coincidentally, it's the **pressure** that we must first address in order to perform well on an exam. You've got to ease your anxiety as you prepare for the test and while you're taking the test so that you can focus and take care of business. You can start by training yourself to adopt a positive perspective. You might think this is silly, but honestly, when you put a negative spin on things, you're already setting the stage for something bad to happen. In other words, if you think the test is going to be impossible, you'll be more likely to give up or not put forth your best effort. So change "this exam is going to be hard" to "this exam is going to be a challenge," and then challenge yourself to step up to the plate.

When you're really confident, you don't even think of exams as exams. It's simply an exercise, like homework, or even a crossword puzzle. Think of it like this – if you're a basketball player shooting a foul shot, it really shouldn't matter if you're in practice or in a game. The ball is still round and the foul line is still the same distance from the basket. So athletes who understand the power of positive thinking can block out all of the crowd noise and the pressure, and shoot the ball just like they do in practice, even if it's really the championship game with a tie score and no time left on the clock. They face the pressure through focus, the same as a concert violinist or a Broadway actress does. They've gone through the routine hundreds of times before. The only difference come "show time" is that they're in front of a crowd. In their minds, however, there is no difference.

How do you get to this level? The first key is to **block out any negative thoughts or apprehensions**. Don't think that you'll do poorly. Even on a subconscious level, it's important to push away doubts. College is going to have its difficult moments for everyone, not just you. The way we overcome them is by thinking positively and successfully doing the next step, which is to **prepare**.

In high school track, we ran. Then we ran some more. When we got tired, we kept running. We learned the basics about running form and breathing techniques, then we did a variety of warm-ups and stretches to prepare our bodies. Afterwards we worked on different skills we would need (speed, distance, etc.), then we practiced running our particular events. So as an 800 meter runner (2 laps around the track), I ran several 800s in practice. These were timed to measure progress. Later, we practiced beyond our events. Instead of running an 800, I would run a 1200 (3 laps) or a mile (4 laps). From this preparation method, I learned the following things: **1) Make sure your form is correct**, **2) Always warm up**, **3) Practice like it's "game time,"** and **4) Proper preparation goes** *beyond* **what's required**.

I chose this simple analogy because when I first looked back at it several years ago, I realized that it paralleled many events in my life. Initially I didn't really enjoy track, but once I did, I began to take practice much more seriously and I did well in competition. On the flipside, I loved basketball but for some reason, I rarely practiced like it was a game. I didn't work on skills that I knew needed improvement. Consequently, I rarely got off the bench.

Schoolwork followed the same pattern. There were some courses that I studied inside and out, either because I enjoyed the material, or I motivated myself to put forth the effort. I usually did well on exams for those classes, and often times, knew going into the test that I would be good to go. In other courses when I didn't prepare well, either due to lack of motivation or poor time management, I only did well on the exams that were relatively simple. And trust me, there weren't many of those.

The next section gives specific recommendations using the 4-step model outlined above. Afterwards we'll look at some "Test Day Tips," discuss strategies for different types of exam questions (essays, multiple-choice, problems), then talk about some things you'll want to do after the exam is over.

Exam Prep Step One: Make sure your form is correct

This step comes into play way before you get into the true exam preparation phase. Who helps an athlete with their form? The coaching staff. Who helps you? The professor, teaching assistant, tutor, and possibly classmates who really understand what's going on. This is why office hours, asking questions during and after class, and tutoring sessions are important. You must make sure that you follow along and understand what's going on. If you misinterpret something or are confused, you might jump to incorrect conclusions which will leave you lost. When something doesn't make sense, ask someone for help.

There's one other important piece to this step. You must make sure your form (or your study techniques) match the type of exam you'll be seeing. When the exam is a few weeks away, make sure the professor talks about it in class. They should let you know approximately how many questions there will be, what kinds of questions (short answer, multiple choice, etc), and which material will be covered. This will tell you what to study and how to study it. If they don't voluntarily give up this information, ask them in class.

Exam Prep Step Two: The Warm-up

This is another step that comes before you prepare for the test. Your warm-up is the **Formula for Success**, broken down in Chapter 6, which includes going to class, paying attention, and reviewing. You're gathering tools and information so that you can prepare to practice (study), and eventually compete (take the test)

In track, specific warm-up drills help you improve a certain aspect of your performance. You might do some high-knee jogs, or focus on lengthening your stride. As you study throughout the semester, things like taking good notes and completing your homework assignments are your warm-up drills, exposing you to different skills you'll need come exam time.

Exam Prep Step Three: Practice like it's "game time"

When a big track meet was coming up, we shifted our practice sessions slightly to prepare for the event. The same is true for you and your exams. You should have been studying over the course of the semester, but now that an exam is approaching, you'll want to focus more attention on getting ready.

When you should start preparing and how much time you'll spend will vary on the type of class, the type of exam, the amount of material covered, and your own learning rate. Starting earlier is always better than not giving yourself enough time, especially if you didn't do as well as you could have on a previous exam in the course. Here are some more suggestions to help you get ready:

- **Take exams.** The best way to get over exam anxieties and prepare yourself is to take exams. Get old exams and go through them thoroughly. Do a practice round or two initially, maybe talking through problems in a study group. Then take a few old exams as if they were tests. Time yourself and correct them afterwards. If you don't have old exams available, create your own. Pull questions from homework sets, quizzes, or the book. Ask the professor for some sample questions that you can work on. Create short-answer and essay questions from your readings and notes, then answer them, again in a test environment. Once you go into the actual test, you should feel more comfortable.

- **Don't half-step.** If you don't understand a certain topic, don't just hope that it won't appear on the exam because Murphy's Law says that it will. This is another reason to study early and often so that you don't get to a confusing concept the night before an exam and be out of luck. The sooner you see it, the more help you can get.

- **Adjust your form.** As you study, critique your skills. Are you taking too long to work through problems? Are your essay question answers too wordy? Are there still some things that you don't get? Make the necessary adjustments to stay on top of your game.

- **Make your notecard (formula card) early.** For some courses, such as science or math classes, the professor will allow you to bring in your own card of formulas. Do not wait until the night before the exam to make this card! Create it while you're studying and use it to solve problems. This will get you used to working with it and also let you know when you've forgotten to include something. When making your card, write small, but write neatly. Also, if you have space, squeeze in other information that may help you solve difficult problems.

- **Preparing for open book or open notes exams.** Finding out an exam is open book or open notes doesn't mean that you don't have to study. Make sure you can efficiently use your text and notes by knowing where to find stuff. Students who don't prepare for these types of exams will spend more time flipping through pages than answering questions. To be honest, if you prepare well, you probably won't even need to look at your book or notes much.

Exam Prep Step Four: Go beyond the minimum.

Here's the deal. You have a certain amount of time to prepare for an exam. Once you sit down with your pen or pencil in hand, and put your name on that exam paper, there's nothing else that you can do. Your goal is to enter the exam with as much knowledge and confidence as possible. If you half-step through practice (your exam preparation), it will show. If you push yourself, it will show. You're not going to magically earn an "A." You must do the work required of you, then do even more.

Two days before the exam, revisit Prep Step Three above and honestly ask yourself whether you've done all that you could do. Did you skip any sections or topics because you didn't understand them? If so, go back and ask someone to help you. Did you do enough problems? Do more. Make your practice tests harder than the real test. If you do this, the real test should be absolutely no problem for you. That's the mentality you have to strive for.

The Day Before the Exam

- **Rest.** We didn't run wild the day before a track meet because we needed our energy. You train harder earlier, then rest before the race. This is a difficult concept for college students to apply to courses because you think that you must use every available second before the test to cram. If you plan a better approach and manage your time, you can avoid the all-nighters. Many of you will probably still struggle with this for the simple fact that there are only 24 hours in a day. Try to get as much rest as possible, but if you need to put in more time to review, do what you have to do. You'll know when you know enough, and hopefully as your college career progresses, you'll figure out how to learn more sooner.

- **Pack what you need.** You don't want to be rummaging around your dorm room looking for your calculator the morning of an exam. Pack you backpack the night before with whatever tools you need – pens, pencils, notecard, book, notebook, calculator, watch, etc. Also, if your exam is early, put a snackbar and a drink in your bag to eat on the way in the morning.

Exam Day

- **Wake up.** This step is pretty important. Set an alarm or two. Have a friend call you or get mom to do it. Whatever you need to do, make sure you rise with enough time to get dressed, get focused, and get to class.
- **Eat something.** Don't take an exam on an empty stomach. But don't go to the All-You-Can-Eat buffet either.
- **Where is it?** Sometimes exams won't be in your normal classroom. Make sure you know in advance where the test is going to be given, and that you know how to get to that building. Factor in extra travel time if needed.
- **Get there a few minutes early.** It's much better than being a few minutes late.
- **Relax.** You've studied. You've paid attention. You know what you're doing. So there's nothing to be worried about. Just get ready to show what you know.
- **Write it down.** Once you get the exam sheet, take a minute to write down any stuff that's swimming in your head that you think you might forget. Use the margin or the back of the page.
- **Name and date.** Handle that before you get too busy.
- **Preview the test.** Quickly browse through the questions. Look for stuff that looks familiar and easy. Note the variety of questions. Quickly gauge which sections look like they'll take longer.

- **Read the instructions.** Don't skip this step! What if the instructions say to answer any two of the following five essay questions, but you skip over this and answer all five. You've just wasted valuable time and you won't be getting extra credit.
- **Do the easy ones first.** Answer the questions that you know, or do the sections that will take you less time. You don't have to start with question number one.
- **Watch the clock.** Bring a watch or use your cell phone if it keeps time, in case the classroom doesn't have a clock. Watch your time on the overall exam, and for individual questions. If something is taking too long, skip it then return to it later.
- **Use the test.** There may be something from a particular question that will help you figure out another one, so look for that information and use it to your advantage.
- **Check your work.** You'll be tempted to turn in your exam and get it out of your life once you're done, but if you have time left over, go back and look over your work. You don't want to get penalized for simple mistakes, and you'll hate yourself if you skip this step and lose points. Whenever possible, always try to finish an exam with at least a few minutes to spare so that you can look things over.
- **Don't do it!** We've all been tempted to peek over someone's should or whisper to a neighbor for an answer. But think about it…is trying to get a few more points really worth risking everything? Colleges have cracked down much harder on cheating, so don't give anyone a reason to suspect you of anything. Focus on your own work, otherwise risk getting a zero for the exam, failing the course, or even getting kicked out of school.

Exam Types

- **Essay Questions.** Be succinct, but clear. You don't have a lot of time, so there's no need to be overly wordy. But be sure to write complete sentences, instead of phrases or fragments. Also, make sure you're answering the question that was asked – if it says "compare," do a comparison. If it asks for your opinion, give it. If you have to explain something, then break it down. It's always good to incorporate ideas from the class readings, lectures, or other related concepts. Finally, watch your time and write neatly.

- **Multiple Choice.** Answer the question in your head *before* you look at the multiple choice selections. Hopefully the answer you came up with is one of the choices. Look at all of the choices carefully, and pick the *best* fit. If you're stuck, cross out the ones you know definitely aren't correct. Be careful of choice A – it's often a trick answer that may seem right, especially if you're rushing. Don't spend too much time on a particular question. Come back to it later.

- **True/False.** Read the question carefully. Be mindful of extremes such as *Always, Never, Only, Best, Worst,* etc. These statements are often false, since one counter-example will prove them wrong.

- **Problem Solving.** If you must show your work on the test, make sure to write clearly so you can earn partial credit if you don't get the correct answer. If you're using your own scratch paper, still write clearly and keep your work organized so that you can easily re-trace steps if you need to. Reviewing your work is very important here. You don't want to lose points for simple math errors. Also watch your time, because you can easily get caught up in a difficult problem and leave little time for the rest of the exam.

- **Take-home exams.** These don't have the same pressure and constraints of an in-class exam, but can still be difficult. You may be expected to put in a lot of research into a take-home essay, solve difficult problems, or sort through loads of information. Often a poor performance on a take-home is the result of not devoting enough time or waiting until the last minute, so clear out your schedule and take care of business.

- **The difference between midterms and finals.** Nothing. An exam is an exam. If you slack on a midterm you'll only be putting more pressure on yourself to get an "A" on the final.

After the exam

You've just left a very difficult exam. You're going through the usual array of emotions – relieved that it's over and hopeful that you wrote down enough for those few questions you weren't sure about. If you didn't prepare well, you'll probably be quite annoyed with yourself because you know if you would have put more time in, you could have done better. What's done is done now, however. You've probably got work for other classes to catch up on, so handle that, but also keep a few things in mind for future exams, and for when you get this one back:

- **Adjust your preparation.** If the style of the test threw you off, or you were simply under-prepared, make a list of the things you can do differently next time and start sooner. If you're unclear on how to make improvements, speak with the professor about the best approaches to studying for the next exam.

- **Keep your prep materials.** Hold onto your formula card, old exams you had been going through, notes, etc. You may be able to use those for the final exam, or in a continuation of the course next semester.

- **Check the grading.** When you get your test back, make sure you received credit for all of your correct answers and that the total adds up to the score you were given. Check the things that were marked wrong and make sure they actually were incorrect. If you believe that you got something right – fully or partially – make note of it. For an essay or short answer question, maybe your point differed a bit from the answer the professor was looking for, but was still valid. If you have any sort of problem with your test score, respectfully approach the instructor after class or during office hours and explain the situation. Make sure you have a valid claim, however. Don't ask for a higher grade simply because you don't appreciate the "C" they gave you (which you, coincidentally, probably earned).

Summary

Exam preparation is your final run through of the material, not your first time seeing it. Maintain a mentality for success and use a thorough studying process to stay caught up with the material. In other words, make it easy on yourself by using your resources and efficiently organizing your information throughout the semester, then study it hard, going beyond what's required at exam time. You should never be in the dark about how well you did on an exam. If you prepare properly, you'll leave the test with the same confidence that you had coming in.

TEN. TIME MANAGEMENT: FROM BIG PICTURE TO SMALL TASKS

Manage your time. Don't let it manage you.

Suppose you've read through all of the chapters thus far and have restructured your academic regimen so that you're going to use all of the best possible techniques. Or maybe you already had it together and knew how to study effectively. Now suppose that your time management skills are so terrible that you never make time to open your books. You could be the smartest, most potentially studious person on campus and flunk out of school before your next fashion show rehearsal, Drama Club meeting, or football game. And sadly, you wouldn't be the first one.

Many of the difficulties that students face on campus have nothing to do with intellectual ability. They simply get caught up in other things and don't make effective use of their time. Some of the by-products of this include waiting too long to start assignments or prepare for exams, falling behind in coursework, and not making time to use help resources. Further, students can end up in a dangerous cycle of under-achievement and ensuing frustration, which can cause them to study even less.

You must manage your time and discipline yourself so that you take care of your schoolwork. You can't simply ride the wave and be down for whatever, whenever. You need to establish a personal schedule that enables you to effectively balance academics with activities, and future ambitions with current obligations. To do this, you need to **prioritize**, **set goals**, **plan your time** to achieve those goals, then **make sure to follow the plan**. You must also be able to think about **long-term** goals and plans, as well as **short-term**. The idea is to use your long-term items as a starting point for your short-term planning. Let's break it all down and see how it's done...

Making your Long-Term Plan

The first thing to understand about "long-term" is that it's all relative. For a freshman who knows they want to be a doctor, long-term may be nearly ten years away, once they've finished undergrad, med school, and their residency. For someone else, long-term may mean next year, or even next month. It really all depends on the context and scope. Since this book deals with college, our basic framework for long-term, in the longest sense, will be your four (or more) years of college and the year after you graduate, as you make the next transition.

Your long-term planning will not be nearly as detailed as your short-term for the simple fact that we can't predict the future. You certainly want to lay out some goals and options, but you probably won't have all the logistics ironed out. Still, long-term planning is an important part of the process because it puts things on the map and gives you something to shoot for. As time goes by, your long-term items will eventually become "right now" activities and be factored into your short-term planning.

Here's an example to better illustrate the point: It's first semester, sophomore year. After your freshman year you went back home for the summer and worked at your old high school job at the mall. You realize for this coming summer, before junior year, you want to get an internship in your field of study. This is a long-term goal which may not be worked on much fall semester. In the spring semester, however, with summer right around the corner, it's time to get cracking. Tasks related to what began as a long-term objective now appear on your short-term "to do" lists – research internship options, put together and send out résumés, make follow-up calls, buy a suit for interviews, etc. But if you're really thinking ahead, you might start typing your résumé during a slow time in the fall semester (you can always fine tune it later), and plan on getting a new suit for Christmas (better someone else's money than your own!).

An effective long-term map can help you make informed decisions, take short-cuts, start things sooner, and create beneficial opportunities. The more you know about what you want to pursue or accomplish in the long-term, the better you can prepare yourself.

The format and approach you use to establish a long-term strategy can vary greatly, and is really up to what fits your style and needs. I've kept journal entries, lists of goals, New Year's resolutions, and prospective timelines looking at things such as academic and career options, relationship goals, travel plans, places I wanted to live, fitness plans, writing schedules, and much more. Spend some time thinking about where you see yourself next year and in the next five years. If you're really feeling bold, go ten years out. What do you want to get out of sophomore year? How do you want to make senior year different than junior year? Think about what you want to do and where you want to be, then run through some options that will take you there. Write it down and hold onto it. You'll need to refer back to this later.

Making your semester plan

Your semester plan is a specialized short and long-term projection that will be critical to your success. At the beginning of each semester, once your course schedule is resolved and your various activities have begun, take some time to map out everything that's going on. The idea is to get a clear snapshot of your entire semester so that you can effectively prioritize and plan.

Start with your goals. What do you hope to accomplish this term? What grades are you shooting for in each of your courses? What do you want to get out of the activities and student groups you're in? Are you trying to lose weight or eat better? Do you want to visit home more often, or save up a certain amount of cash? Think of other areas you're working on or goals you want to set, then make your list.

Next, create a semester chart. Sometimes they'll be available for free via some sort of campus promotion. Or you can buy a nice wall-sized version at the bookstore or an office supply store. You can also make your own or use the template available at our website (www.lionsstory.org/college). The chart enables you to **see the whole semester at a glance**. This is much more effective than viewing a month at a time.

On the chart, fill in every important date you can think of – exams (midterms and finals), due dates for papers and projects, athletic events, organization responsibilities, student group performances, breaks and birthdays, appointments, application and registration deadlines, conferences or other travel plans, and anything else that's relevant to your life. Obviously you won't know everything now, but whatever you are aware of, write it down. As you find out about new events, such as a concert you want to go to next month, or as things change, like an exam date being pushed back, make the change to your schedule.

Now pull out your long-term notes from whenever you last spent some time with them. Also look at the semester goals you've set and your semester chart. What do you see? Is your chart so full of activities and events that your semester grade goals may be in jeopardy? Do you have enough open days before your midterms and finals to study effectively? Where are the crazy points in your schedule (2 papers and an exam all in the same week), and how are you going to tackle them? What things are within your control that you can adjust if need be? Can you go away for spring break or will your workload be picking up? When can you make time to start researching grad school programs? Have you factored in any time to work on a long-term goal or two?

Answering questions such as these will help you make a realistic semester plan. If you need to adjust your time table, do it. Maybe one of your courses is too much right now and you need to find something with a lighter workload, or take four classes instead of five. Maybe your activity schedule is too hectic and should be scaled down. Don't be afraid to make the necessary changes. Making choices to prevent potentially stressful and wasteful situations may be a difficult decision, but it's much better to proactively address concerns than pay the cost later.

Making your short-term plan

A short-term plan can come in a number of formats, but will typically focus on a weekly overview and a more detailed daily "to do" list. To help you get to that point, a good place to start is with a **Weekly Timetable Grid** (or, for my technology people, your Static Schedule).

This is similar to the semester chart from the previous section, except this time we want to break down what your typical week will look like. You can create the grid yourself, listing the days at the top of the page, and the hours down the left hand side. Write it out on paper or type it on computer so that you can re-use it each semester. You can also download our basic grid template from our website.

Once you've got the grid in hand, fill in the time blocks that will be consistent for you this semester. Map out class and lab times, your work hours, meeting times, practice times, and other things that are scheduled daily. Don't forget to include your workout schedule and times to eat. If you don't schedule it, it may not happen.

Now look back at your semester goals and your long-term objectives, then take a real close look at your grid again. Where are the open time blocks for studying and tutoring? Identify them and mark them off. Now ask yourself, is this going to be enough? What were your grade goals again? Can you reach them with this study schedule? Do you need to shift some things around (wake up earlier and study, adjust your course schedule, cut something out)?

Once you've optimized the schedule and made sure that the time available for studying and activities effectively matches the goals you've set, you will then use this weekly time grid as your working model. Each day, however, there will be various new and exciting things to do, such as a Friday gathering with friends or an Entrepreneurial Club guest speaker. You'll also have a host of uneventful tasks that you must take care of, like laundry, food shopping, and graduate school applications. This is where your **Weekly/Daily Planner** comes into play (also known as your Dynamic Schedule).

Again, the format you use is completely up to you. Some people like fancy daily planning books, others will just need a simple to-do list. You want to spend some time on Sunday looking at the entire week ahead of you, then throughout the week, review and update the day-to-day events. You may also want to take note of some things you'll be doing *next* week, just to keep them in mind. This process will help you better manage your time and spread things out. You can always adjust the plan as the week goes by.

To start, look at your semester chart and your weekly time grid. What exams and projects are coming up? Map out your study schedule for the week to give you enough time to prepare. What about that campus event you want to go to on Wednesday evening? Do you have the time to spare? Do you need to cut your gym time down on Thursday, or switch from Thursday to Friday this week so you can take care of something else? What phone calls do you need to return and when are you doing it? And when are you going take care of that pile of dirty clothes?

Before you know it, any open spots in your weekly grid will quickly be filled by various daily tasks and events. Planning it out will help you keep everything in perspective and effectively make use of your time, instead of wondering where the time went and why you haven't gotten anything done.

Making it work

Now this is the million dollar question. How do you make your plan work? Your schedule says you're supposed to go the gym three times a week. So why haven't you been in a month? You had a four-hour study block yesterday, but you only put a good hour in. What happened?

Life happened, that's what. All kinds of things will come up to throw you off schedule. You've got to remain conscious of this and make sound decisions that will keep you out of time management trouble. Here are some things that can help:

- **Keep the plan visible.** I ran into a slew of time management issues simply because after mapping out my plan, I failed to look at it often enough and would forget to do things. Check both your long-term and daily plans so that you remember what you're supposed to be doing. It's a good idea to look at the daily plan in the morning to see what needs to be done, then review it at night to make sure you covered everything, and make adjustments for the next day.

- **Don't over plan.** Be realistic with your time scheduling. Don't schedule to do more than you can actually accomplish in a given amount of time. Space things out, whenever possible, to allow for things to run over. And factor in travel time and prep time. Over planning will just throw off today's schedule, and possibly tomorrow's as well. Also don't over plan by spending too much time scheduling stuff and not enough time doing it.

- **Specialize your study times.** When you first do your weekly timetable, you want to identify open spaces in your schedule when you can study. Think about each course you're taking and the amount of hours required, then try to designate your study time blocks accordingly. For example, if you have a big chunk in the middle of the day on Wednesdays, study for a class that needs more time. Also consider time of day and other personal factors – if you do problems better than you read at night, set aside those times for math.

- **Give and take.** There are going to be times when you'll have to focus harder on a particular course, like when you have an exam or project coming up. Adjust your study schedule, but also think about how to recover in your other courses as soon as possible.
- **Me, Myself, and I.** You must remember that these three individuals are really one in the same. As much as I wanted to, I couldn't be in three places at once. But I could...
- **Multitask.** If you make a point of it, you can do a bunch of things at one time, like plan your schedule while you watch the game, do some light online research and e-mail people, and preview or review class material while eating lunch.
- **Minimize procrastination.** This is easier said than done, but do what you can to cut this down. Change locations, study something else, or take care of something more interesting on your to do list. Wasted time can't be recovered.
- **Push yourself to do more sooner.** Waiting until the last minute may not be so much a lack of time, but more a lack of will power. Stop putting it off. Lighten the last minute load by starting today.
- **Know what you're getting into.** Make sure you know how long things are going to take. If someone invites you to "Career Day" and they're driving, you need to know if you're staying for an hour or do they literally mean career *day*.
- **Prioritize on the fly.** Be careful of those things that "just come up." Just like you actively participate in class and actively read, you must also actively schedule your life. Think about what's important for you to accomplish then don't get side-tracked by other unplanned or lower-priority events. If your friends want you to hang out but you really can't do it, be strong enough to say so by...
- **Learning to say "no."** It's an easy word to vocalize, but sometimes very difficult to say. Friends who don't have an exam will try to drag you to the party when you need to study. Or one of your organizations may need help with a fundraiser, or a friend may want you to look at a problem they're having with their computer. You'll find that once you get known for something (cooking, hair-braiding, fixing stuff, volunteering, DJ'ing etc.), people will request your skills constantly. Know when to say no. Don't put your academics in jeopardy trying to please other people.

- **Plan downtime.** Some people may argue against this, but I think it's fine to set aside time for socializing or fun. Are you really going to study on a Friday night? Leave that space open and do whatever you want. But also be responsible; if you've got an exam on Monday and you know you're not ready, you better be in the books and not at the party on Friday.

- **No frills.** In college I either cut my own hair or let it grow out because I didn't have time to wait in the barbershop every other week. Ladies, your make-up routine may have to be put on pause and you might want to invest in a hat or two, or get used to the pull-back ponytail. Look for other time-consuming luxuries that you can reduce or eliminate.

- **Don't sleep.** Watch the extensive afternoon naps or those Sundays when you're eating waffles and eggs at 2:00 PM. Staying up late will throw off your sleep pattern and make you tired during the day. Try to sleep on a regular schedule so that your body will be refreshed and let you take care of what you need to do.

- **Check your "relations."** Those of you involved in relationships face a wide range of potential time management issues. When it's just starting, you spend hours on the phone or around each other. When it's about to blow up, you spend even more hours arguing and chasing each other around campus. Who plugs this into their schedule? No one. So now you're taking away from class time, study time, sleep time and throwing everything off. Be careful.

- **Refine your game plan.** Each day, if you're paying attention, you can learn more about yourself. You might find that you like working at your job more in the late afternoons so that you can study in the morning. Or study groups work better than reading after dinner. See what's working and what's not then make adjustments.

- **Be punctual.** When you have an appointment or some place to be, be on time. Better yet, be a few minutes early. This will help you maintain a positive outlook about time management and also relieve the stress and tension you may feel as a result of always running late.

- **Make it a routine.** The best schedule is one that flows on auto-pilot. You're at the gym before class, at your work-study job hours, in class, putting in your study time, then meeting with your study group, all without thinking, because you've established a routine. Once your course schedule is straight, take the next two weeks to put yourself on a daily routine. Try not to deviate from it. This will set the tone for the rest of your semester.

- **Analyze your time.** If your routine just isn't happening, it's time to investigate. Chart how you spend your time over a week – write down when you wake up, what things you do throughout the day and how long each of them takes. Now look back at the way you planned to use your time and assess what's different. Then seriously think about how you can adjust these differences so that you can put your schedule to work.
- **Stay focused.** It's your time and your stuff to get done. If you don't do it today, and do it right, you're just going to have to do it tomorrow. Think about what you need to do and take pride in getting it done.

Making changes

Things in your life are going to change, so everything from your long-term goals to your daily schedule might also adjust. You may change majors, join a new organization, break-up with a long-time boyfriend or girlfriend, or suddenly decide that you want to study abroad next year.

It's important that you remain in tune with yourself and gauge your goals and your plans. Think about what you said you wanted to do, and whether or not you still want to do it. Maybe that idea to jog every morning before class was ahead of it's time. Or maybe you need to push yourself a little harder and put your running shoes on. Self-assessment is the key to self-improvement. When we avoid asking ourselves questions, or fail to honestly answer them, we can lose touch and get off track.

Set aside some quiet time to review your plans and then make whatever changes are necessary to continue moving towards graduation.

Summary

There are twenty-four hours in a day. What we do with them is completely up to us. Often, what we do and what we *can* do vary greatly due to a mismanagement of time.

Nothing in your class schedule should ever be a surprise to you. Life gives us enough unplanned events, so you can't "just remember" that you have a paper due tomorrow. Invest some time into managing your time, prioritizing the things that matter most. Evaluate and update your plans as needed, staying true to yourself in the process.

PART THREE: LIFE ON CAMPUS

ELEVEN. HOME SWEET HOME

For many students, aside from summer camps or time spent with a relative "down south" (seems like we all have some southern family, don't we?) going away to college will probably be your first extended time away from home. Though this transition may initially cause some anxiety, there's nothing to worry about. It doesn't take long to get settled in. Before you know it, you'll be calling your dorm room "home" and the place you used to call home will be known as your "parent's house."

In order to truly make your new house a home, you want to first make sure it's a good fit, then you want to do your best to fit in. Each year of college offers new living opportunities. Typically you'll be able to choose where you want to live and who you want to live with, though sometimes your choices will be limited. For example, many freshmen are placed in on-campus freshmen housing with a random roommate. Even for upperclassmen, options may be slim on certain campuses. Whatever selections are available to you, be sure to choose wisely. If, however, you end up in a situation that's beyond your control, try to make the most of it.

It's crucial to your well-being that you maintain a sense of comfort, safety, and support in your dorm room or apartment. College will present enough stressful situations. If your personal space also becomes a stressor, this could pose a serious problem. The rest of this chapter will look at some of the factors to keep in mind regarding your current living situation, and things to think about when it's time to choose next year's housing.

Roommates

Many freshman year living options give you little or no say about who your roommate(s) will be. For some students, this may be your first experience living around someone of another race. And even if you have an African American roommate, their experience and background may be completely different from yours. In all cases, you must enter the situation with an open mind and a positive attitude. You and your roommate(s) don't necessarily have to be best friends, but you do have to get along. Here are some suggestions to get you started:

- **Establish early contact.** If you're provided with your roommates' contact info before school starts, try reaching out to them. Send a letter or e-mail, or get on the phone. You don't have to give them your life story, but let them know a little about yourself – interests, personality, and what you intend on studying. If you end up speaking beforehand, you can even discuss who's bringing what for the room. If you're not able to connect before the school year starts, make it a point to develop a relationship during move-in. Spend some time getting to know each other. Each roommate will be a little nervous at first, but the best way to ease this anxiety is head-on. After all, this stranger is going to be waking up in your room tomorrow. You may as well get to know them.

- **Set up expectations and guidelines.** I used to be the "let's wait and see/hope for the best" type, and still am in some cases, so laying down roommate guidelines always seemed a little too pushy for me. Nevertheless, it's a critical step. If your roommate doesn't know that you don't want them to use your toothpaste, or that they should only squeeze the tube from the bottom, what can you really say? Jokes aside, you don't have to get nitpicky and give them a bullet-pointed memo of regulations, but do spend some time talking through important issues. Does anyone have a boyfriend or girlfriend and what's the protocol for overnight guests? Are you going to have quiet study hours in the room? Can they use your computer? Which one of you is the neat-freak and which is messy – and what are you going to do about this?

- **Respect.** This is always the golden rule. If you're unclear on an expectation, just think about whether or not you're being respectful. Would you feel disrespected if your roommate ate your food, or used your dishes and didn't wash them, or had all of their friends over to play video games while you were trying to study? Always keep in mind that you are sharing a space, and respect the other people who also call that space "home."

- **Make time for each other.** You'll be surprised by how little you may see your roommate as the semester goes on. Between dating and socializing, traveling with the team, classes, working, and studying, you'll often spend more time outside of the room than in it. Or everyone may be around but in their own space or own worlds. If you haven't had a good conversation with your roommate in a while, make time for one. Do lunch once a month, or go to a dorm or campus function together. Try to maintain a bond, but also be mindful to...

- **Give each other space.** You and your roommate may be cool, but remember, each of you also has your own life. They may have other friends or activities, so don't get mad if you're not hanging out all the time.

- **Diverse issues.** Diversity comes in many colors and flavors. You might be saving up coins for a ticket back home for break while your roommate's parents are driving matching Bentleys. You might be from Indiana and your roommate's from India. You might be a conservative living with the next Michael Moore. You could be strictly NYC underground hip-hop while your roommate represents the Dirty South. In short, diversity is not a black-and-white issue, nor is the question of how to effectively deal with it. My advice is to treat people as people first, and learn from your experiences with them. I've lived with people of various races and though I took something away each time, I often feel like I could have learned more. There were so many other people from all over the world whom I crossed paths with daily on campus but never even acknowledged. One of the reasons why we're so ignorant of other cultures and parts of the globe is because we get so caught up in our own lives. On the flipside, exploring diversity sets us up for questions like, "how do you get your hair to do that?" and "do you really think OJ is innocent?" In the classroom, I would pick and choose my battles. Among roommates or people I'm cool with, it was usually not an issue at all. I've asked my share of crazy questions among people I respected, which initiated some great dialogues. If you don't ask, how will you ever find out? And once you do find out, you usually also find a mutual respect and common ground.

- **When problems arise.** Even if you end up being close with your roommates, eventually there will be some sort of conflict. Someone may have left the room messy, had loud friends over too late, or left the door unlocked all day. If you have an issue, don't hold it inside because then it will only bubble over and you may blow up the next time something goes down. This adds unnecessary stress to your life. Instead, respectfully talk it through and try to reach an understanding.

- **The problems aren't going away.** When situations escalate or involve a more serious matter, it's time to seek intervention. Most dorms have a Resident Advisor (RA) whose duty is to help keep the peace. Seek them out and have each person explain their side of the story. If the RA can't propose a viable solution, they may consult outside assistance. In the worst case where roommates absolutely can not work out their differences, most schools have a room switch period or can arrange an emergency housing reassignment.

Get involved

Many college dorms will provide some sort of programming or activities, such as floor meetings, pizza parties, guest speakers, workshops, Secret Santas, movie nights, bowling trips, and more. When your schedule permits, take advantage of these informational or fun events. Also get to know the people on your floor or in your building. Just like with your own roommate, there's no need to cut people off or create unwanted tension. If you brush by your neighbors without speaking, or they do the same, it creates an unwelcome feeling. Most likely, no one will be going anywhere all year, so get involved in your dorm's activities and keep everything cool in the neighborhood. Saying "hi" and "bye" is not that difficult. You can end up developing some close bonds in the process.

Exploring your living options

Usually after your first year of school, your living options widen. You can escape the designated freshman dorms and move anywhere you want, on campus or off. You may also be able to choose your roommates. Here are a few points to consider:

- **Living with friends**. This can be a great experience or it can ruin a friendship. Sometimes people can get too much of each other, plus college is a time of change. The person you knew freshman year may not be the same by junior year. And guess what? That's okay (unless their changes aren't healthy). You have to give them room to grow and respect their choices. In general, before deciding to live with a close friend – or anyone, for that matter – talk out your expectations (paying bills, cleaning, guests, noise levels, etc) and make sure you understand what you're getting into. Just like with any roommate, communication and respect are the keys to making it work.

- **Shacking up**. Deciding to live with a girlfriend or boyfriend carries even more weight than living with a friend. Are you both ready for this? (Even if you say you are, are you really, or are you just saying it because that's what the other person wants to hear). What does this move mean for both or you? For some couples, moving in together is just a way to cut costs, or an issue of convenience. For others, it's a serious step towards marriage. Are you both on the same page with what it means for you? What do your parents think? If your folks are adamantly opposed, it can cause a strain at home, and also potentially in your relationship and your schoolwork. (While we're on the topic of parents, don't think you can keep your living arrangement a secret. Your parents *will* find out sooner or later). Be completely open and up front with each other and with your families before making this move. You don't want to have to break a lease and be scrambling for a new place to live right before midterms.

- **Living alone**. I've never been a big fan of living alone in college. Even though I liked maintaining my personal space, I just didn't like the idea of being by myself all the time, isolated in a box. For me, college was about building relationships, so I typically lived with at least one other person. Having a roommate not only helped my peace of mind, but drastically cut my living expenses, especially off-campus during grad school. Some people, however, feel like living alone is the best way to stay focused. They may enjoy being around people but want to retreat to a space all their own at the end of the day. If you know that's what you want, then definitely pursue that option. Two things to keep in mind, though. Depression on college campuses is a much bigger issue than people discuss (we'll talk more about this later), and it can set in much faster and deeper when we cut ourselves off. Secondly, ladies, be very careful when living alone. Make sure you keep your doors and windows locked, and be wary of who you invite over.

- **Room and Dorm types.** Some dorms may offer apartment style living with separate bedrooms, a bathroom, kitchen area, and living room. Others will have the more traditional dorm setup – 2 beds, 2 desks, and 2 dressers all in one room, with a bathroom down the hall. Most dorm rooms house 1-4 people, depending on their layout. A large off-campus house can hold even more. Some dorms will be single-sex buildings or floors and others will be mixed. Each may offer different services and facilities such as a dining hall, fitness area, or computer lab.

- **On-campus living-learning programs**. Many schools have living-learning communities which focus on specific themes. Students involved in these programs will all live on the same wing or floor, or perhaps even share a whole building, and focus on technology, business development, Spanish, African American culture, the arts, or numerous other areas of interest. These programs often host speakers and functions centered around their theme. This is a perfect chance to live among like minds and extend your learning outside of the classroom. See what kinds of programs your school has to offer. If none are available, or you don't see what you're looking for, consider starting something informally, or even seeking a faculty advisor and developing your own program.

- **Becoming a Resident Advisor (RA)**. If you're financially strapped and enjoy giving back to the residential community, this may be the move for you. At many schools, RAs live rent-free or receive some other perks. Don't just do it for the money, though. You have to be interested in supporting your residents and helping foster the community spirit. When someone from your floor comes knocking at your door at 3:00 AM with an emergency, remember, this is the trade-off. This is part of your job.

- **Moving off-campus**. There're a bunch of factors to consider before making this move. First of all, it's OFF campus, which usually means farther away. How far are you willing to go? How will your daily schedule be affected now that you have to factor in more travel time to and from home? I know people that moved off-campus and suffered because they were too lazy to walk to class. Another point to consider is money. Your off-campus rent may seem like a bargain, but don't forget about the utilities (heat, water, electric, phone, cable, internet, etc). Most of these things are bundled into on-campus living, but you don't find out about them off-campus until after the fact. You also will need to get together a security deposit, first month's, and often last month's rent before signing a lease, which can be a nice chunk of change. And after all of that, now you have to get furniture (which is provided free on campus). Get some advice from people who currently live off-campus before making your move. Check out the landlords, too. If possible, deal with someone who has a good reputation and is familiar with college students. Sign your lease for a year only. Don't lock yourself into a bad deal. Read through the lease, too. Look for clauses about pets, subletting, smoking, etc. Finally, this may seem like a trivial thing, but remember, you have to invest time into finding a place to live, which usually takes longer for off-campus housing. Don't be lazy about this, because you're picking the place where you're going to lay your head for a whole year.

- **Moving to a fraternity or sorority house**. For some of you, this may be a dream come true. For others, it may be a bit too much. Will living in "the house" be too great of a distraction? Or perhaps this is the activity that you really want to put your heart into, thus living in the house will give you the most satisfaction. Whether or not you end up living with your brothers or sisters, you're still a part of the organization. You have to decide what living arrangements work best for you.

- **Commuting**. If your school is near your home (or a relative's house), it may make sense for you to commute. I know students who decided to do this in order to save money or because they felt their grades were suffering and wanted to distance themselves from campus life. Commuting usually requires you to shift the way you think about school, almost like it's a job that you go to every day and not a lifestyle and culture that you're always a part of.

Summary

One of your missions on campus is to create a living environment that supports the goals you've set for yourself, along with your individual sanity. Take some time to figure out the best living situation, making sure to take advantage of the various resources and programs that your school and/or off campus communities have to offer. Prevent common roommate problems through communication and respect, but as conflicts creep up, address them quickly. Most of all, enjoy shaping your own space on campus, meeting new people, and getting involved in the many residential activities available to you.

TWELVE. STAYING ORGANIZED, CLEAN, AND VIRUS-FREE

It's amazing the things you learn when you're living on your own. Who knew that laundry detergent costs so much or that leftover spaghetti sauce in the fridge will eventually grow mold? Why didn't anyone tell you that no matter how long you iron that shirt, it will never come out crisp like when mom hooked it up? And where exactly are you supposed to store a year's supply of plastic forks?

Welcome to college.

This chapter will take a look at some of the things you'll need to think about as you get settled in and begin your brand new "independent lifestyle."

What to bring and where to put it

Honestly, you shouldn't bring a whole lot. First of all, you're not going to have much space to work with. Secondly, you probably won't use half the stuff you bring. If you forget something important you can always get it over break, have it shipped, buy a new one, or simply hold out 'til next year.

Keeping it simple is the best rule. Did you wear all of your clothes in high school? Then don't bring them all to college. Here are some more tips:

- **Check the landscape.** Usually on-campus housing will provide you with the basics, so you won't need to bring your bed, just the sheets. Some rooms may have kitchenettes, microwaves, bathrooms, living rooms, etc., so find out your setup beforehand then plan accordingly. For example, if you have your own bathroom, you'll need your own toilet paper and cleaning supplies. If the bathroom is down the hall, invest in shower shoes and a bathrobe.

- **Stock up on school supplies.** If you plan to do a lot of studying in your room, you want to make your workspace as comfortable and functional as possible. Get a desk lamp, note pads, pens, stack trays to keep your papers and mail organized, and anything else that will help you get the job done and keep the clutter limited.

- **Stock up on storage bins, too.** These are truly a gift of the gods. They come in all shapes and sizes and work well on the bookshelf, in the closet, or my personal favorite, under the bed. Store your coins, old school work, clothes, cleaning supplies, CDs, books, and the all-important "miscellaneous items."

- **Buy in bulk.** If you do have some extra space in your room, it's a good idea to make a run to the wholesale store with the folks and go "economy-sized" on the stuff you'll need. This way they won't worry about you not having any soap, and you won't have to spend your own money.

- **Off-campus furnishings.** If you have an off-campus apartment, I have one word for you – USED. Buy as much secondhand stuff as possible because you're not taking it with you when you graduate.

- **Create your own system.** You have to know where your stuff is – important papers, money, class assignments, etc. Keep it organized instead of letting it pile up all over the place.

- **Think "multifunction."** Since your computer also plays CDs, you can leave the stereo at home. You can go a step further and get a TV card for your computer (only recommended if you're in a room that has a cable connection) and leave the TV home, too. Most computers also play DVDs, and the newer flat panel monitors give you even more free space!

- **Work it out.** If you and your roommate share one room, or there are common spaces in your suite such as a living room or closet space, think about how you want to divvy it up. Don't take up all the space and leave them with none. You must also agree whether to maintain a certain level of cleanliness in the entire room, or whether your half is yours and theirs is theirs. But truthfully, you should...

- **Keep it clean.** There's really no excuse to live in a dump. Of course if you have an exam tomorrow you're not going to be worried about dusting and window-washing, but during your downtimes, try to keep your environment reasonably straight. Also, every now and then, take some time to go through all of the junk that you've accumulated and get rid of some of it. This may help you create some order in your space.

- **Leave the valuables at home.** Dorm rooms really aren't the most secure places. If you've got something that you don't want to lose, find a safe, secret place to store it, or leave it with your folks.

- **Kick the habit.** If you've got a video game addiction, then you might want to leave the game system at home, too. Nobody wants to hear about how you can stop whenever you want. Your grades won't lie.

Wash and Wear

So, you're new around the laundry room, huh? Don't worry, it will be our secret. There's not that much to it, really, so here it goes:

- **Powder or liquid?** It doesn't really matter which kind of detergent you use. I like liquid, because the container is sturdier. I had a box of powder detergent bust open once, so I had to make the switch. But they're both soap, so use whatcha got.
- **Read the labels.** When it says "Dry Clean Only" it means dry clean only. Don't put it in the washing machine. Take it to the cleaners. "Wash separately" has some leeway, though. You might want to wash it separately the first time, then throw it in with like colors on future washes. But if you want to be absolutely on the safe side, just do what it tells you.
- **Separate your stuff.** Do colors in one load, whites in another. Otherwise you'll end up with pink t-shirts, which you probably don't want. Wash colors, especially dark colors, in cold water so the colors don't bleed. Whites can be done with warm or hot (though I've heard hot is actually overkill; most things are fine with warm). Do your own tests and see what works best.
- **Inside out and empty your pockets.** Turn t-shirts with logos or writing and sweaters inside out when washing. This will keep them looking newer longer. Also, before washing, check your pockets for slips of paper, lipstick, money, etc.
- **Play favorites.** There will be some machines in your laundry room that just don't get the job done. Older washers may have rust spots inside and mark up your whites. Some dryers may require you to run them twice before fully drying your clothes. Once you find machines that work for you, stick with them, whenever possible.
- **Don't over stuff.** You've gotta leave some room for the clothes to spin around in the washer and dryer. You may think

you're saving money by cramming them full, but you'll only end up having to wash or dry your stuff again.

- **Prompt removal.** Don't leave your clothes in the dryer overnight. For starters, it's disrespectful. Other people need to use the machines. Secondly, you're leaving yourself open to getting your stuff stolen. Thirdly, you'll be lucky to only spend a few hours ironing all the wrinkles out. And definitely don't leave your clothes in the washing machine overnight. You have heard of mold and mildew, right?

- **Other people's stuff.** In a shared laundry space, it's typically okay etiquette to remove someone else's clothes from a dryer once the final cycle is done, and place them on top of the machine, or on a nearby table if available. Some students may get offended by this, and even have something smart to say. If you don't want people touching your clothes, don't let them sit in the machine all day.

- **Use off-peak hours.** If you think you'll be washing your clothes on Saturday or Sunday afternoon, think again. You'll have to take a number, along with the rest of the folks in your building. Try early on the weekends, between classes, or some other low-demand time.

- **Put the iron down.** I was never a fan of ironing so I avoided it whenever possible. One trick is to neatly fold and hang your clothes right when they come out of the dryer. Don't let them sit all piled up in a basket or on your bed all day, or just throw them any old place. Another trick is to hang a slightly wrinkled piece of clothing in the bathroom when you take a hot shower. The steam may get some of the wrinkles out.

- **Pull the plug.** When you do have to break the iron out, unplug it when you're done. If it's unplugged, it's off, even if you forgot to turn it off. This is something my folks taught me that I still do to this day.

- **Store your off-season stuff.** I learned this one from women. Fellas, pay attention. You have what are called "summer clothes" and "winter clothes." When it gets too hot to wear your sweaters, fold them, put them in a storage bin, and slide them under your bed or put them in a closet somewhere. This frees up shelf and rack space in your clothes closet, keeping things organized. Don't pack up all of your sweatshirts in the spring, though, in case you don't like air conditioning, or for those cool evening walks along the beach...or to the library.

Computer Blues

Technology is a big thing, not just in college, but practically everywhere. When your parents are e-mailing you instead of calling, you know the world is changing.

Do you absolutely need a computer on campus? My gut instinct says yes, simply because I'm a computer person and can't function long without one. If you can't afford your own machine, however, most schools have labs that you can use. In either case, you need to be smart when you rely on technology, because viruses, glitches, and simple human error can wipe out all of your saved data, and even your computer. Having to reformat your machine is not a fun experience.

- **Save often.** This is a fundamental step that still snags many students. Save as you type, not after hours of work. Your computer could freeze, the power could go out, or some other act of technology may erase everything but your pain.

- **Back it up.** Another basic element of computing. What are you going to do when you lose that disk labeled "Important Files. Don't Lose." Burn backup CDs of your important data in case your computer crashes or you misplace a disk.

- **Learn to type.** The one-finger-at-a-time method is really a big waste of time, especially if you're using the computer a lot.

- **Use protection.** Computer viruses are no joke these days. If you don't have at least an up-to-date antivirus program on your computer, it's only a matter of time before you get hit. And when you do, you could end up having to reinstall everything on your computer.

- **Bring (and save) your original disks.** Computers can break down, with or without a virus. You may need to install a driver or reinstall a whole application, so make sure you don't leave your disks at your parents' house or lose them somewhere in your dorm room.

- **On or off?** If you're not paying for electricity then there's really no need to turn your computer off. Set the screensaver to launch or the monitor to go to sleep. Technically-savvy students will use their computer as a file server to store their stuff, and will want to be able to access it via the network throughout the day. The only real danger in leaving your machine on is that if it's not properly protected, it could get hacked.

Because technology changes so rapidly, we chose to maintain more tips on our website so that we can give you the latest updates. Visit www.lionsstory.org/college for more information, including tips on what kind of machine to buy, how to prevent hacking, and more.

Summary

Bring only what you'll need to college (including your clothes and your computer), and keep everything organized and clean.

THIRTEEN. JOIN THE CLUB: ACTIVITIES AND ATHLETICS

Activities and organizations on campus, from your dorm's social planning committee to a varsity athletic team, are arguably the essence of the collegiate experience. They provide opportunities for students to extend their education beyond the classroom, becoming more well-rounded and self-aware along the way. Most schools offer a wide range of activities to choose from. Often, self-determined students will come together and create their own group if they can't find what they're looking for.

For African American students, organizations can have an ever deeper meaning. Many groups are tied to a rich cultural or school legacy, such as the renowned marching band of an HBCU, fraternities and sororities, Black Student Unions, choirs, and other similar groups. African American students may also have a more positive overall campus experience by becoming involved in organizations, as this helps them create a connection to the campus and a broader sense of purpose.

Why join?

Students will find themselves drawn to groups and organizations for a wide variety of reasons. For some, it will be a natural continuation of a skill or activity they've pursued since high school or earlier, while in other cases, a student may want to dive into something brand new. Other students will want to explore networking and pre-professional opportunities, or enhance their leadership skills.

Many future employers and graduate schools look for multi-talented students who were active in campus groups, so being a part of an organization certainly won't hurt in that area. Ideally, your reasons for participating should go beyond simply enhancing your résumé, however. For me, groups initially represented a chance to meet new people, have fun, and add some variety to my campus routine. As I became more active, I saw opportunities to not only expand my own experiences, but to leave a mark on the university and community, and leave something behind for the students to come after me.

During my time in college, we affected change on many levels and through a variety of means, some of which were quite unexpected. For example, I was a part of the planning committee for an intramural football league comprised of predominantly African American students. This league, called "The Du Bois Bowl," literally became an institution on campus, and included over 100 students in its peak seasons, male and female. For many African American males, playing in the Du Bois Bowl on autumn weekends was their connection to Penn. Ironically, one of the driving forces that started the league was an influx of Black males who had unfulfilling experiences with Penn's varsity football program. Instead of becoming disillusioned, they created their own playing field.

Other students also played key roles in changing the face of the campus. One established an African Drum and Dance Troupe which is still thriving and has performed throughout Philadelphia. Another single-handedly guided the African American campus newspaper when no one else wanted to carry the torch. There are numerous other individual and group stories which demonstrate the possibilities available to those who have vision and determination. Possibly the most valuable lesson I learned about activities on campus is that with an idea and some legwork, you can make just about anything happen. We'll talk more about this in a moment. First, let's look at what you'll have to choose from.

Types of organizations on campus

The number of activities available to you will typically depend on the size of your campus, though many smaller schools also offer a wide range of student activities. Students attending predominantly white institutions will not only have numerous groups catering to Black students, such as the Black Student Union, but will also have clubs and organizations for all students, like Student Government, the school band, and the school newspaper. Some organizations will have national ties, such as the National Society of Black Engineers (NSBE), a college chapter of the NAACP, or a sorority, while others will be campus-based. Membership can also vary, from a handful of students to a few hundred, in the case of a school marching band.

The following is a breakdown of some of the things that may be available:

- **Social, Political, and Service Groups.** This includes organizations such as Student Government, tutoring and mentoring groups, fraternities and sororities, the Black Student Union, Gay/Lesbian organizations, and others.
- **Cultural Groups.** Depending on your school's population you may have groups such as a Chinese Student Association, Caribbean Club, or programs celebrating Jewish heritage.
- **Performing Arts Groups.** A variety of options may be available such as dance groups, drama clubs, singing groups, poetry collectives, hip-hop groups, and more.
- **Academic and Pre-professional Groups.** Organizations such as an honor society, a technology or business club, NSBE, or SNMA would fall under this category.
- **Athletics.** This includes varsity athletics, club sports, and intramural teams.

The above listing gives you a basic feel for the various options. Some groups, such as the Black Student Union or a fraternity may heavily engage in more than one category. For example, a frat may host a Black history series which would be cultural, sponsor a hip-hop step show which would fall under performing arts, and host a career seminar which would be pre-professional. The categories here simply serve as starting point. Look into the groups available on your campus and learn more about their programs and mission so that you know what best fits your interests.

Leading a group

As you move up from freshman to senior some of you will also rise from general member to president of a group on campus. Or you may have begun your own organization and be the leader by default. Regardless of the circumstances, understand that you have a tremendous opportunity ahead of you, not to mention a hefty amount of responsibility.

Student leadership adds a host of new tasks to your semester schedule, but ultimately should prove to be one of your most memorable and rewarding experiences. Your time management skills will be tested, so remember, if you're going to invest time into something, be sure to get something out of it. In other words, do your best to make sure that your organization is successful under your watch, and that you remain on track for your personal goals. Here are some suggestions which you can incorporate:

- **Learn from the past.** Connect with the outgoing leadership as much as possible. Find out what worked and what didn't. Make sure you know where important organization files and supplies are. Get the past leader's forwarding contact info and don't be afraid to call them with questions once you're in charge.

- **Set goals, make a plan.** Just as you do for yourself, you must also set organizational goals then create a plan for achieving them. Don't limit your focus to just this year. Think about where you see your organization in the long-term as well as the short. This will help give direction to future leaders which they can mold and shape. Also, get input from the group regarding the goals and plan, then make the final goals known to all. This keeps everyone informed and on the same page.

- **Delegate.** This was always my biggest problems early on in my leadership career. If you want something done right, you don't necessarily have to do it yourself if you can effectively communicate the mission and build a level of trust. I rarely took the time to clearly outline project details to others, nor did I look to them for advice or assistance. The next thing I knew, I had way too many things to do. Eventually I ended up either spreading myself too thin and burning out, or half-doing things, which is ultimately pretty pointless. Why not just let someone else do it in that case? I finally saw the light and did just that. Your organization members and the other people on your board or leadership team are there because they believe in the group and want to be a part of the action. If they begin to feel like useless spectators, they'll eventually lose interest. Spread the work so that everyone plays a part in the organization's operation and development. If you do this successfully, you will also...

- **Find future leaders.** Many organizations suffer and even die because once a dynamic senior leader leaves, no one else picks up the ball. Or if new leadership is in place, they may not have an idea of what they're supposed to be doing, and end up starting things from scratch. As a leader, your responsibility is to guide the organization and turn it over to capable and well-prepared hands once you step down. Identify people from your board and membership who have the interest and potential to lead next year, then include them in the process early on. Designate a transition or turn-over period where the outgoing leadership trains next year's heads. Sometimes capable individuals may not even be thinking about leading the group, so you may have to first plant the seed. That's exactly what happened to me when a few seniors, including the outgoing leader, said to me, "you'd make a great NSBE president next year." Maybe it was all a big plot to gas my head up, but it worked. I have since successfully employed this very same technique many times myself.

- **Lead from within.** You don't have to be the president or chairperson to be a leader. If you're on the planning committee or executive board, or even if you're simply in the general membership, you can still be an effective leader. Take ownership of the organization and voice your opinions. Step up and volunteer for projects and assignments. Propose your own ideas and initiatives. Groups thrive when they don't rely on one person to carry all of the weight.

- **Lead by example.** The best leaders will inspire others when they are just being themselves. Understand that as a group leader, you will be in the spotlight. Some people will talk about you no matter what you do, but don't give them any fuel. Back up your words with action, and represent the organization and yourself with class.

- **Solidify the foundation.** Many organizations have a rich history which can easily be forgotten in the shuffle of leadership changes and busy events calendars. Look through the archives, connect with alums and faculty advisors to get a good picture of where the organization came from and how it has evolved. Former members and leadership, old and recent, can be an important resource and help keep the organization connected to its mission, so don't exclude them from the equation.

- **Monitor the group and yourself.** Take some time periodically to assess what the group has accomplished and ensure that everything is still functioning well. Do the same for yourself. Maintain a healthy balance between your leadership responsibilities and your individual school duties. There are going to be challenging times, but be careful not to overburden yourself. At the end of the day, if your poor grades keep you out of school, your activities will also be put on hold.

The bigger picture, the downside of student groups, and potential turnarounds.

It's very possible that an active African American student may be a part of a performing arts group, a pre-professional organization, a sorority or fraternity, and an honor society, all while holding down a work-study job and taking five classes. Additionally, you might find one student leading two or three different student organizations.

From an organizational perspective, oftentimes various student groups may depend on the same over-stretched student body to be active members when they simply don't have the time or energy to commit. Or three different groups may host events on the same night and essentially cancel each other out.

This is the part of the story that's often not discussed. What do you do when organizations are draining students more than benefiting them, or have become ineffective, or no longer fulfill their stated purpose?

Step back and think about the big picture for a moment. Student groups are supposed to provide a service. But when you're dealing with a group of individuals who have other rigorous demands, you need to think about what makes the most sense, not simply from an individual or organizational standpoint, but from the whole community's perspective. In other words, how can the collective body of African American organizations effectively provide services to its audience without overburdening its workforce (which coincidentally, is also the audience)? This is a difficult question and may have even more difficult answers.

Organizations pride themselves on autonomy, history, and presence, however, it may benefit the organization and the student body to have events co-sponsored by several organizations and not just one. This means that your single organization can't take all the credit, but it should ensure a larger attendance, ease the planning workload, and possibly enable a larger scale production. Another suggestion is to create an events calendar for all of the African American groups on campus. This takes planning and communication, but reduces scheduling conflicts and promotes co-sponsorship. Finally, student groups need to establish broader and more responsible goals that incorporate collective success. If you know some of your group members are having problems in their classes or don't manage their time well, do you still keep them in rehearsal until 11:00 PM or later? Do you address academics at all in your group's goals? Do you require a minimum GPA to be a part of the group, and is this enforced? Do you encourage and support each other? Can all Black groups on campus join forces to set academic standards and develop an academic excellence plan?

Here's an idea – have an ongoing friendly competition between all of the African American groups on campus. Whichever group has the highest membership GPA at the end of each term gets some sort of award. Or within your own group, have a contest among each class. One of the roadblocks to doing something like this is that people may not want to divulge their grades. And this is exactly the climate that you must change. When students have a grade sheet full of C's, D's, F's, and Incompletes, of course they want to keep this a secret. But if your group actively promotes a rigid study routine, as outlined in the Formula for Success, and sets a minimum GPA standard, then you should see more A's and B's. If a group member does fall below the minimum GPA, encourage them and motivate them until they pick things back up. This is the type of peer support that can truly change the way people approach their schoolwork.

These steps are not difficult to implement, it's simply a matter of understanding their importance and then making the change. If you already have an umbrella committee of various group leaders on campus, then you have taken the first step. If not, organize a monthly or semesterly "meeting of the minds" – African American group leaders, interested students, and faculty or alumni advisors – and discuss the organizational climate on your campus. Talk about what's good, what's bad, and how you can ensure that everyone has a more positive academic and extracurricular experience. In my view, as a leader of Black students, this is your foremost mission.

Giving Back and Building Bridges

Every African American student should consider some sort of community service work during their time in school. I say this not only because my area of research is centered around service and educational development, but because I truly believe in the benefits of students working with others, particularly younger African Americans. If you're a part of an organization, or a group leader, look into establishing a community service component within your organization – adopt a school, host SAT and college application workshops, set up a weekly tutoring program, etc. Or as an individual student you can look into mentoring programs, Big Brother/Big Sister, coaching a youth league, or other opportunities. Finally, if you have younger siblings, cousins, or kids in your neighborhood back home, talk to them about your experiences at school. Many kids may dream of college but have no idea of what it's really like. Others may not even be thinking about it and can benefit from your personal experiences and stories. A simple conversation or a weekly tutoring session with a 9th grader can truly change their life...and yours.

Notes for Student Athletes

Participating in competitive sports while in college is a tremendous honor. You'll get the opportunity to continue improving your skills, develop strong bonds with your teammates and coaches, and have some of the best times of your life, on and off the field or court. Being a student athlete is also a huge commitment. College is already difficult enough, but combining it with the pressures, traveling, and time constraints of college athletics only multiplies the challenges you'll face.

The bigger the school, the bigger the sport, and the bigger your role on the team, the more pressure and scrutiny you'll face. Imagine being a Big-Ten starting quarterback, or the center of the women's basketball team, or an Olympic-hopeful track star with your picture in the school paper every week. When you're winning, everyone on campus will greet you with a smile and words of praise. But when things aren't going so well, you may feel like never leaving your room. Athletics on all levels can bring out the best and worst in people. Keep that in mind and take things in stride. Very few teams go undefeated, so you'll have some good days and some bad ones.

Finally, one of the biggest challenges for student athletes will be time management. No matter the size of your school or the popularity of your sport, you'll be expected to train and practice, attend team meetings, and compete against other schools. Between classes and your team responsibilities, you may have very little time in your daily schedule for much else. You must discipline yourself to use your time wisely. The first word in student athlete is *student*, so you're expected to preview your lessons, go to classes, review right after, do your homework, keep caught up, use your resources, and effectively prepare for exams just like everyone else. Use the tips below to help you with your time management and your sport, so that you can be an all-around success.

- **Talk to your professors.** Let your instructors know that you're on a team and may be absent for certain class sessions. They should offer tips for making up the missed material, and may even provide you with notes or other resources that you can use.
- **Get a class buddy.** Link up with a student in each of your classes who can fill you in on what you've missed. Get missed notes, explanations of material, and form a study group to regularly go over the material.
- **Balance.** Be careful not to let sports take up your whole life. Try to make time for other interests, even if it's just a few moments or an occasional escape. Definitely don't let sports overshadow your schoolwork. Most college athletes will not make it to the pros, and even if you've got the talent and confidence to go to the next level, an injury could unfortunately set you back. Take your degree seriously and plan on putting it to use.
- **Act responsibly.** We've all seen the movies where the college football team is drinking kegs at a post-game party, flipping cars over, and creating a ruckus. Or we've heard the news reports about student athletes accepting illegal gifts, causing themselves and their schools embarrassment. Don't let your sports fame (real or imagined) go to your head,

especially when it clouds your judgment. Student athletes can and do get kicked off teams for foolish behavior. Others face legal trouble. Some, like one of my childhood hoops idols, Maryland star Len Bias, pay with their life. Bias died of a cocaine-induced heart attack in 1986, the day after he was the second player chosen in the NBA draft. Please, be smart.

- **Practice like you play.** Put your all into your sport during practice then reap the rewards come game time. If you put forth a good effort in your sport, the positive energy should carry over to the classroom.

Summary

Student groups offer an excellent opportunity to meet new people, become exposed to valuable information, and even develop your leadership skills. Many business, political, and community leaders started out running a student group on campus. When becoming involved in organizations and activities, whether you're the president or a freshman member, be sure to manage your time wisely and maintain balance. Organizations themselves also need to focus on the big picture and ensure that they're meeting the academic and social needs of the students.

Get involved in at least one organization or club during your college career. You may not have a good initial reason – you may have noticed a flyer or be dragged to a meeting by a friend. Sometimes chance situations such as this can open you up to the most rewarding experiences.

FOURTEEN. EVENTS ON AND OFF CAMPUS

Pick a day, any day, and I'll bet there's some kind of event happening on campus. Even during final exams, one group will sponsor a "Study Marathon" while someone else is hosting a "Study Break." And back in the day, if there was pizza being served, then best believe I'd probably be checking out both.

Quite a few big names were featured speakers at Penn, such as Maya Angelou, Spike Lee, Chuck D., Terry McMillan, Haki Madhubuti, Henry Louis Gates, Jr., Goodie Mob, Toni Morrison, Danny Glover and Randall Robinson. There were many many others. And of course there were smaller scale functions such as workshops on getting ready for grad school, panel discussions on sexual health issues or the legacy of Black fraternities and sororities. There were also floor meetings in the dorm, Poetry Cafes, "Soul Food Sundays," Kwanzaa ceremonies, movie nights, Black History Jeopardy, and more. All of these were opportunities to learn something new, get valuable information, share ideas and laughter, meet new people, and simply unwind after a long day of classes and studying.

Take advantage of the events and programs happening on campus, and don't limit your focus. Look through the school newspaper, online calendar, and at the various flyers around campus and see what grabs your attention. It might be a presentation on yoga, financial management, graphic design, study skills, careers in the music industry, or ancient Egyptian philosophy. Whatever it is, if you have the time, check it out. After all, your tuition paid for it.

You should especially go to events that relate to your major, or have the potential to help you after graduation. For example, if you're pre-med and there's a panel on "How to Get into Med School," you should be there. Or perhaps you intend to pursue a career in journalism, and Susan Taylor of *Essence* magazine is going to be a keynote speaker at your school. Make it a point to schedule this in. Getting information is not the only reason these events are attractive. You'd be surprised just how accessible people are at many functions. Often there will be a Q&A session or a reception before or after, where you may have the opportunity to meet the keynote speaker and network.

Be in charge
Another way to gain networking opportunities is to get on a planning committee. Not only will you meet the speaker, but you may also decide who the speaker will be. Find out which groups sponsor campus activities, then see about getting involved. Or if you're already a part of a group on campus, suggest your ideas to the group leadership or take the lead on putting together your own activity – maybe a health forum or a Black business panel discussion. If you have an idea, or don't like what you're currently getting, don't just sit there. Get with the program, then put the program together yourself.

Events off campus
Whether your school is located in a major city or a small town, spend some time getting to know the surrounding community. If your school is near other colleges, you may want to stay abreast of their programming calendars. Also find out what there is to see in town – are there any historical or cultural sites, shopping districts, or hot night spots? Maybe there's a biking trail or a pro sports team? A park, a comedy club, or a restaurant that reminds you of home? Step off campus and explore your surroundings for a change of pace and scenery.

Summary: Make the time by making a plan
You may be wondering when exactly you'll have all of this free time to explore the city and take in the various on-campus festivities. Well, there are three ways to go about this. You can either 1) Do whatever you want to do whenever you feel like it (i.e., hang out all the time) and watch your grades suffer, 2) Mismanage your time and become overwhelmed with school work to the point where you have to pass on much of the social stuff, or 3) Effectively map out your time, taking into consideration important events and activities, then follow through on your planning.

Option three is not always easy. You may underestimate your schedule and get thrown off, or you might find out about an important event a few hours before it starts. Try your best to stick to your plan, and most of all, prioritize. If you've got things to do and a campus event is more of a time risk than a benefit, skip it. There will be other functions on other days.

FIFTEEN. THE J-O-B: WORKING WHILE IN SCHOOL

Working while in school can provide you with some extra cash, stress relief from your coursework, valuable experience, and even connections to possible full-time employment leads. Most campuses have a wide range of jobs available for students, such as stacking books at the library, assisting at the recreation center, researching for a professor, monitoring computer operations, or helping in an administrative capacity. You want to make sure that you find the right job to fit your needs.

There are three basic schools of thought to choosing a job. You either want to **1) Maximize your time**, **2) Maximize your cash**, or **3) Maximize your experience**. If you're lucky, you can find something that fits more than one bill.

Maximizing your time

Being an engineer, plus being active in several organizations, time was always my number one issue. I didn't have much of it to play with. I needed a job where I could get my schoolwork done and get paid in the process. To me, that was the truest meaning of "work-study." So I chose to be a monitor (and eventually manager) in the computer lab in my dormitory. It was convenient, flexible, and stress-free. Plus I was essentially getting paid to do my homework, which was certainly a win-win in my book.

Maximizing your cash

You're not going to make your first million off of your campus pay rate. Also, federal work-study regulations limit you to working a maximum of twenty hours per week during the school year. Students looking to earn bigger bucks may choose to work off-campus, such as in a department store, where they can work longer hours. Or you may have your own side hustle. You can do hair, be a DJ, promote parties, take pictures, design websites, tutor, make t-shirts, cater events, do income taxes, sell real estate, or numerous other options. Just make certain to save some time and energy for your schoolwork.

Maximizing your experience

If you're going to medical school after college, you want to get a good lab job in undergrad, or tutor in the sciences. If you want to be a sociologist, look for a job in the sociology department, or become an assistant or researcher for a professor. Get paid to get ahead. Your boss can be an excellent mentor and recommendation writer, and may have connections with grad schools or companies which will help you get your foot in the door.

Should you work?

Before you start looking for a job, you want to answer this question. If you've received a work-study grant in your financial aid package, put it to use. If you didn't, you may be able to find a non-work-study job or work off campus. Many jobs, on and off campus, will understand that you're a student and offer flexible scheduling opportunities. In some cases you can make a week-to-week schedule, or commit to only working a few hours each week. If your course schedule is light, then consider working more hours. However, if you're really nervous about taking on too many responsibilities in school, put off working until sophomore year or wait until you're comfortable with campus life, then start sifting through the job listings.

Getting a job

Check with your school's employment office for a list of the various jobs available on campus. This information may also be on your school's website. Also check the school newspaper and look around for job flyers, especially the first few weeks of school. Before you settle on something, ask around for other options. Talk to upperclassmen, faculty, and staff at various departments. If you want to work in the athletic department, go down there and see what's available. Sometimes the employment listings won't be up-to-date.

Everyone will want to hire you the first week of school, but do a good search and have some options to choose from. Somebody, somewhere is getting paid to do something that you're doing for free. Take your time looking, but don't take too long, else you might miss out on a good opportunity.

Keeping your job (this year)

Yes, you're in college, but once you accept a job, you have to honor your commitment to that job (even if you stayed out until 4:00 AM the night before). Take your job seriously and display professional courtesy. Show up when you're supposed to and do what you're getting paid to do. Even if the job is pretty basic, don't blow it off, or think you can study the whole time. Remember, it's still a job, and you can be fired.

Keeping your job (next year)

You're not obligated to remain in the same job each year. You may want a different experience, a different work schedule, or simply a change of pace. If you have a good rapport with your employers, let them know that you'll be moving on next year. In some cases, turnover is built into the job and your bosses won't even count on your return. If you want to keep your job next year, make sure everyone is on the same page.

Summer gigs and quick hookups

If you'll be around campus for the summer, look into what jobs are available. Often campuses sponsor a variety of summer programs and will need counselors and coordinators. These positions may come with free housing or other benefits. Additionally, at Penn, students could volunteer to assist during move-in and move-out. Some of these positions were paid, but all enabled student workers to move into their on-campus housing early (or stay longer, in the case of move-out). This is a great way to ease transitional housing stress.

Also, put some thought into your summer planning. You may need to make more money in the summer or get in some good work experience. Can you afford to take an unpaid internship? Do you need to go home and save up your cash? Look at all the factors before making a decision.

Summary

Your job on campus should be a good compliment to your overall experience. Ideally you should enjoy what you're doing and ultimately benefit from it, whether it be paid study time, much-needed income, or experience and connections. Look into all of the jobs available, including summer and temporary positions, and once you're hired, be respectful and professional in the workplace.

SIXTEEN. MIND, BODY, AND SPIRIT

So far we've discussed identity and goal-setting. We've looked at study skills and test-taking strategies in great depth. We've talked about time management, living situations, and getting involved in activities outside of class. Now we're going to talk about the glue that holds it all together. You.

With so many things to grab your time and attention it's very easy to let your health go. But if you neglect your body, your mental health, or your spiritual foundation, you may run into serious problems. Take some time to read through this chapter so you will know the signs and possible solutions. Also, pay attention to the proactive strategies for maintaining a healthy lifestyle and an optimistic outlook.

>> Diet

At the start of my very first summer school session, I hadn't yet found a job so my pockets were a little light. I decided to go on a self-designed "super money saver diet." There was a pizza place around the corner from me that had an on-going special – two large pepperonis for ten bucks. I ate pizza for breakfast, lunch, and dinner for almost a month. I figured I had all the food groups covered, right? *Wrong*. And unfortunately, I neglected to factor in the "excess grease" group. Then I had the nerve to wonder why my stomach didn't feel right half the time.

Many of you will sleep through breakfast, grab something unhealthy for lunch, then have to skip dinner due to an evening class followed by a meeting or study session. After mistreating and malnourishing your body, you still expect it to hold out for you until the wee hours of the morning, day in and day out. At some point, something's going to give.

According to the Center for Disease Control and Prevention, the number one killer of African Americans in 2001 was cardiovascular disease (CVD), which relates to high blood pressure, heart disease, and strokes.[1] Number five on the list was diabetes.[2] Neither of these illnesses are instantaneous, but are spurred by years of poor eating habits and limited exercise. As I've mentioned several times in this book, you must think both **long-term** and **short-term**. Yes, the potato chips in the lobby vending machine will provide you with a quick and cheap fix, but if this becomes your pattern, what will be the cost down the line?

Taking control of your health now will reduce the risk of major illnesses in the future, and more immediately, it will give your body what it needs to make it through a long day and an even longer semester. To get started, look into the following:

- **Eat right.** This is where it all starts. Eat a variety of foods to nourish your body, not simply satisfy a hunger or craving. Don't always settle for what's convenient if it's not good for you. Break unhealthy habits and check out the Food Pyramid on www.lionsstory.org/college for a daily listing of what you need. Also try to eat smaller meals throughout the day, and keep the late night food fests to a minimum, especially if you're trying to lose weight.

- **Don't skip breakfast.** You may have just woken up and not done anything yet, but you haven't eaten since yesterday, probably 8-10 hours ago! You need to refuel your body and get it ready for the day, otherwise you'll be running on empty and will feel sluggish and fatigued.

- **Check out the cafeteria.** Most school cafeterias aren't as bad as the stereotype makes them out. Many are actually quite health-conscious. From a time management perspective, the cafeteria is a good choice (no cooking or clean up for you), but if yours really isn't to your liking, petition to get things changed. It's there to serve you, so put it to work!

- **Going for self.** If you decide to cook some or all of your meals, look on the internet or in cookbooks for healthy recipes for a busy lifestyle. We have a few things to start you off on our website, www.lionsstory.org/college. Many meals don't take that long to prepare. Read the labels when you do your shopping so you know what you're getting (additives, fats, carbs, calories, etc). Also, think about going back to basics and packing your own lunches. A turkey sandwich with lettuce and tomato on grain bread, along with some fruit and a water or juice is a great alternative to the burger, fries, and soda combo meal.

- **Vegetarian, anyone?** There are a variety of diet and lifestyle options that you can choose from. Some of you may have been raised on a vegetarian diet, while others may become interested in trying new eating habits while in school. Whatever you decide, do your research to make sure that you get the right balance of nutrients.
- **What to avoid or cut down.** Many of you probably don't want to read this, because unfortunately a lot of the tasty stuff that we're used to, such as fried foods, cheese, chips, cookies, sodas and coffee are not doing anything good for us. They are filled with sugar, cholesterol, saturated fat, salt, and caffeine, which are linked to numerous short and long-term issues.
- **Intensive weight loss programs.** Recent statistics indicate that 64% of African Americans are overweight.[3] Some will turn to popular weight loss programs or dietary supplements, and expect unrealistic immediate results. Weight loss is a lifestyle change that involves overhauling your diet and incorporating regular exercise. Thoroughly research any weight loss program before beginning it and don't get discouraged if the pounds don't drop right away. You have to stick with it! Also be wary of any program that promises weight loss but doesn't include any physical activity and/or allows you to eat whatever you want.
- **The importance of water.** Your body is made of about 70% water and depends on it to function properly. Additionally, drinking your 8 glasses of water each day can help you fight fatigue, boost your memory, and even reduce the risk of cancer.[4] Water is also crucial to weight loss. Instead of eating, drink a glass of water next time you're hungry for a snack, especially late at night. And remember, a "serving" of water is only 8 ounces, so if you make it a habit to carry around a 32oz. bottle and sip throughout the day, you'll get half the water you need without even realizing it.

>> Exercise

You only get one body, and trust me, as you get older it doesn't get any easier to take care of it. Develop a healthy program of eating right and exercising while you're in school, so that it becomes a part of your lifestyle.

You may not be into the whole gym thing or jogging, and that's fine. There are many more options to choose from. You can fast walk, play tennis, swim, or bike. You can also look into taking a class if you need more structure to stay motivated. Many school recreation programs will offer a variety of cardiovascular courses, from spinning and step aerobics to forms of dance. They may also have personal training options to get you started in the gym and help you develop a customized program.

Exercising can do just as much for your mind as it does for your body. It's a great stress relief, and as you drop pounds and tone up, you'll gain self-confidence. Working out can also provide a greater sense of daily accomplishment. It's something that many of us put down on our New Year's resolutions, but quickly brush to the side when things get hectic. Staying with it produces results and a feeling of personal investment which can carry over to other aspects of your life.

Here are some tips to help you stick with your program and make the most of your fitness experience:

- **Make it a routine.** Whatever you do, try to do it at the same time, on the same days, 3-5 times per week. Treat it like a class. Once you break out of your pattern, it's difficult to get back in gear. Find something you like and some times that work and stick with it. But if it gets boring...

- **Try something new.** If you're lifting weights, try a different workout routine. If you've been running, take a different course, or give swimming a try. Sometimes we don't get turned off by the idea of working out, but more by our chosen format. Experiment with different activities and identify a few that can hold your interest.

- **Take advantage of the free stuff.** Your school may sponsor free fitness courses, personal training sessions, a jogging club, intramural sports, or other activities. These are great ways to stay active, meet people, and have fun. And most of this "free" stuff was paid for by your tuition money, so go sign up for something.

- **Don't be afraid to dig in your pockets.** If there's something you really want to do, or something that you feel will get you closer to your fitness goals, like joining a gym or a weight loss club, or hiring a trainer, check your budget and see if it's possible. Think of it as an investment in your future.

- **Bring a friend.** Working out with a partner will motivate you to show up (you don't want to leave them hanging) and encourage you to push yourself (you don't want to always be the one lifting the lighter weights, looking all out of breath). Exercising with your boyfriend or girlfriend can be a great relationship-building activity that provides some healthy fun.

- **Set goals.** To keep moving forward, set goals for your workout sessions. Run a little longer on the treadmill or increase the weight on your bench press. If you want to go all out, you can develop your own rigorous program and chart your target points and results after each session.

- **Watch the gym stereotypes.** Fellas, there's more to working out than biceps, shoulders, abs, and chest. Don't forget the legs, back, and cardio. Ladies, there are some good free-weight exercises waiting for you, so don't be intimidated. You won't turn to 100% muscle from using the dumbbells.

>> Sleeping

The National Sleep Foundation recommends that you use your bedroom only for sleep and sex.[5] These people take their sleep (and sex) seriously! While this suggestion is not going to be possible for the average college student, who does their studying, eating, computing, entertaining, and sleeping all in one room, you do need to recognize the importance of giving your body sufficient rest.

We all know that a lack of sleep can cause issues (if you don't know, you'll find out soon enough when you're trying to keep your eyes open in class). But did you also know that you can sleep too much? Overloading on sleep is not just a time management problem, but can also leave you still feeling tired and uninspired. Additionally, it could be a sign of depression. Try to establish a regular daily sleeping pattern and stick to it as much as possible. Again, this may be difficult while in school, but shoot for 6-8 hours each night, with regular night time and morning routines. If you need to, consider short power naps in the afternoon. Research shows that these "siestas" can leave you feeling refreshed and actually boost your productivity. (I've been trying to tell people about this for years!)

>> Depression, Stress, and Mental and Emotional Health

We're all going to face problems and challenges throughout our lifetimes. Some issues will be in response to situations we've created, such as stretching ourselves too thin or making a poor decision. Other times we may have to deal with things beyond our control, like the death or illness of a family member or friend. Coping can be an arduous process, but it is the only way that we can begin to heal.

Your college career will oftentimes seem like a headfirst dive into the deep-end of stress. You'll have to absorb book-loads of information in a short amount of time. You'll face the pressures of multiple exams and assignments due in the same week. You'll have friends or family needing advice, while student organizations vie for your remaining free time. Later, you'll be faced with grad school and career decisions, while still holding down a full college schedule. Sometimes it's better to not have any spare moments, otherwise you may actually realize all of the things that you have going on in your life. There will be times when you'll want to press "stop" or at least put things on "pause," but feel like your world has spun beyond your control.

When we let our issues fester, or when things become too difficult for us to deal with, we can sink into depression. Many students experience periods of sadness, confusion, and a general sense of dissatisfaction about where they're headed or where they've recently been. Most of us have had a bitter break-up or a fight with a friend, uncertainties about our academics or financial situation, problems back home, job-search frustrations, or other personal battles. It's quite common to have a down period, even though we try our hardest to front like everything is always cool. If not treated, however, depression can become a very frightening situation, even life-threatening. It's crucial that we don't second-guess ourselves and that we seek help when we feel like things are slipping. The suggestions below offer some tips to prevent this from happening, and some information to keep in mind just in case you do need to reach out for someone.

- **Talk it out.** Your problem may seem difficult and very personal, but speak with someone that you trust. You're never alone, so don't struggle silently by yourself. Talking things through is a way of releasing some of the tension and beginning the search for answers.
- **Stay connected.** In order to talk about your situation, you need to have someone to speak to. Don't cut people off when you're going through something, especially the people that care about you. This is one of the most important reasons to have a mentor, develop friendships, and make meaningful connections. We all need a shoulder to lean on sometimes.
- **Keep a journal.** Recording your thoughts is an excellent way to begin addressing any personal issues. Write about your high points, low points, and even typical days. When you're going through something, journaling can sometimes take your mind off of it, or can be a starting point for working through the situation.
- **Take a time out.** Often we may feel uneasy or tense because we've virtually run ourselves into the ground trying to do too many things. When we reach this point, the smallest disagreement or problem can ignite into an inferno. Slow down. Relax. Breathe easy. Take some time for yourself – a few moments, an afternoon, a weekend – to reset and regroup. Meditate, journal, go for a walk, or just watch some TV. On a bigger scale, this is why it's good to leave campus for school breaks. We all need that time to do something different and fun in an environment free of stress and daily schedules.
- **Develop a feel-good formula.** Whenever you're feeling a little down, put on a favorite CD, watch a DVD that picks you up, call a friend to hang out, or go outside and read a book. Maybe you have a favorite restaurant or coffee shop, or maybe working out or shooting hoops at the gym is your release. Sometimes even dressing up can make you feel better. Have something positive that you can turn to so that you can...
- **Avoid abuse.** Abuse comes in many forms – alcohol, drugs, sex, shopping splurges, food, and even remaining in an unhealthy relationship. You may feel like the pain or the truth is

too difficult to face, and seek an escape. You may not even realize that you're doing this, or be in denial. But if you take a few moments to really think about it, chances are your escapes will always be temporary, and the root of the problem will still be staring you in your face. How long can you continue running and hurting yourself?

- **Look for signs.** Recognize when you're feeling down. Don't brush things off or ignore them and hope they go away. Have you been sleeping more? Have you been keeping to yourself, not really feeling like getting involved with anything? Has your schoolwork and your motivation slipped? The sooner you can take an honest look in the mirror, the better off you will be. Watch your friends' backs too – they may be going through their own issues and be silently reaching out to you.

- **Seek help.** It's hard to admit to yourself that you may need to seek professional counseling, but it's important to get over that stigma and take the first step. Most schools offer counseling and support services because they're essential. These resources are confidential, and should be thought of as nothing more than having a conversation with someone who's trained to help you work through your problems. It's like office hours for life, so instead of searching for excuses, go speak with someone so that you can get back to where you belong.

- **One day at a time.** Each day of life is truly a blessing and a gift. You may be going through something right now, but you're here, and you have the opportunity to do some powerful things. Make the most of each day!

>> Spiritual Health

I always respected students who came from a religious background and maintained their church or mosque attendance, and bible studies or prayer schedules, because in many ways, the rigors and lifestyle of college don't support this. Students may not be able to locate the same denomination as back home, or find a place of worship where they feel comfortable. More often, students struggle with making the time to practice their faith.

For students who aren't very religious, college may be a time for them to explore their spirituality. Because the collegiate environment is one of learning and understanding, often both religious and non-religious students will pose very serious and personal spiritual questions. Students will wonder what can bring them closer to God, and why the world is the way that it is. They may even question the purpose of religions and the very existence of God. These questions are a natural part of the journey that we all take in one form or another. Continue to ask your questions and to develop your spiritual side, but also be mindful of the potential dangers that may be around your campus.

There have been a variety of religious organizations that have made it a point to target spiritually-inquisitive college students. They may lure you with a Bible study or fellowship gathering, but soon make unreasonable demands of you, perhaps requesting money, requiring you to attend numerous functions, or even dictating your friendships, clothing choices, and activities. If you experience a religious group that seems overly aggressive, or simply doesn't sit right with you, respectfully break your ties with them. If this doesn't work, seek advice from a friend, RA, mentor, advisor, or other university administrator.

Most campus religious groups will want nothing more than to help you maintain a solid spiritual foundation and continue to develop as a person of faith. In addition to the various churches and places of worship that may be available near campus, many schools offer faith-based activities such as a gospel choir, while individual students may host weekly Bible studies. Just as with all other activities in college, you must plan and prioritize. You may not be able to make all three Sunday services, sing in every choir, and be a part of the singles ministry, youth ministry, and outreach ministry like you were back home. But you can still participate on a smaller scale, which can provide comfort and support, while also helping to give you confidence and faith in your daily college life. Keep the Lord first in your heart and become all that you were meant to be in the classroom.

Summary

Your health is of the utmost importance, not just in college, but throughout your life. It's crucial that you maintain a healthy balance of proper eating and exercise, while monitoring your stress levels and fatigue. Stay in touch with yourself and seek positive outlets to reduce your tension. Stay connected to others so that you'll always know that you have people on campus who are concerned about your well-being. Stay connected to your spiritual foundation so that you can understand a greater sense of purpose in your life.

Finally, **be mindful of illnesses and colds**, especially during flu season (which always ends up being when you have an exam or paper due). Wash your hands often to keep germs away, and consider getting a flu shot if your school's Student Health Center offers it. If you do end up with a cold or flu bug, it is best to get as much rest as possible and let your body recover, rather than trying to push yourself through the same daily routine. Failing to rest may significantly increase the amount of time that the illness stays with you. If you fear that you have something beyond a simple cold or flu, go to Student Health services immediately.

SEVENTEEN. THE GAME: DATING, RELATIONSHIPS, AND SEXUAL HEALTH

All right, kids, this is the one you've been waiting for. Before we get into it, let's lay a few ground rules. First, the conversation is going to be candid because it has to be. We're dealing with a serious topic, in serious times, but we're all adults so I'm sure you can handle it. Second, you might not agree with everything I have to say. I'm in my thirties, so I'm coming from a "been there, done that" perspective. It's one that I think you need to hear and it should save you from some unnecessary drama, so all that I ask is that you hear me out and then give it some thought. Finally, some of the stuff I'm going to say may seem contradictory. I don't know for sure yet because I haven't started typing, but I just have a feeling that it might go that way. What can I say? That's what this game (and love) can do sometimes. As with everything else in this book, see what relates to your experience and roll with it. Got it? Cool. Let's keep it moving then, starting with **three things that must change in the game**.

Change Number One: We must stop the spread of sexually transmitted diseases and unplanned pregnancies.

I called this chapter "The Game" because relationships often play out like a competition, friendly or not-so-friendly. In the beginning, there's the excitement, the scouting and positioning, and the all-out strategizing. On the strictly innocent level, one person likes the other one so they assess their chances then make their move. Afterwards they wait in agonizing anticipation for a phone call or an e-mail, then talk for hours about everything and nothing, slowly growing what could possibly become a beautiful romance. On the opposite end of the spectrum, the game gets grimy, resembling nothing more than a hunt for new conquests. You're going to get him and her, or steal her man, or sleep with that fly shorty down the hall at whatever cost.

When we shift the focus to sexual health, however, this is where the games have to stop. Your safety and well-being are absolutely nothing to play with.

Men, I don't care how good she looks, whether you've done it before and it was cool, or whatever the story is, do not enter a woman without a condom. Did you hear what I said? *Do not enter.* There is no "I'm just going to put it in for a little while, then put the condom on later." A little while is all it takes to catch something or make a child that you're not ready for. Also save the "it doesn't feel the same with a condom" talk. Damn straight it feels different. It feels like you're going to live to see another day.

Ladies, he may "look like he doesn't have anything" or be someone that you've known for a while. It doesn't matter. Don't let him enter you without a condom. You have the last word on this – don't forget that. If he's not wearing a condom, you need to shut the party down. If he doesn't have one, he can go get one, or you can (and should) keep your own supply. If you're concerned about what he'll say about you for carrying condoms around, think about what you'll tell any future men after you've contracted herpes. If you're worried about ruining the mood, imagine how great of a mood you'll be in when you're five months pregnant and he's seeing someone else.

One third of all college students contract some type of STD by the time they're 24.[1] Unfortunately African Americans are at the top of the list for the worst one, HIV/AIDS. Though we only make up 13% of the total US population, African American women accounted for over 60% of the new AIDS cases in the US in 2003 (African American men were over 40%).[2] In 2001, HIV/AIDS was the seventh leading killer of African Americans.[3] Further, recent reports have indicated an increase of reported HIV cases among African American male college students. This rise is largely the result of what's commonly known as a "down low" lifestyle, or men having sexual relationships with both men and women.[4] The deceptive nature of this the trend, as with all cheating and irresponsible sexual decisions, puts all sexually active individuals at risk. If you're having sex then this includes you, too.

In 2000, there were 1.3 million abortions in the United States, with a large percentage being performed on college-aged women.[5] The social climate on abortion has always been uneasy, and recent political and legal attacks have again questioned women's rights to choose. Most importantly, abortion is a decision you must live with. While you may think it's best to not bring an unplanned baby into the world, choosing to "make the problem go away" might in itself become an issue that stays with you. It's certainly not something to be taken lightly.

Those students who decide not to have an abortion will typically have to take some time off from school in order to care for their child in the early stages. Some of these students do not return. And for those that do, especially if they have little or no help with raising their child, the road to graduation will be that much more difficult.

A simple condom can drastically reduce these concerns, but even this is not a 100% guarantee. Abstinence is still the only sure shot, but is often difficult for college students to commit to. Whatever choices you make must prioritize your health and future. *Yes, it can happen to you.* Believe that! Having unprotected sex puts the life that you know right now in jeopardy. Are a few moments of pleasure really worth the risk?

If you choose to be sexually active, condoms shouldn't be something additional for you to think about. Your mind should already be made up to use one *every single time*.

Change Number Two: We must end the sexual violence against women.

Brothers, this one is all on us. While you can make the argument that women may send mixed messages, or "shouldn't dress like that if they don't want it," your case really ends up being very weak. A woman, or a man for that matter, has the right to change their mind about sex at any point, whether you're about to have sex or are actually engaged in the act. If they say "stop," you stop. Denying their request is an act of aggression, plain and simple. Further, a woman should be able to wear whatever she chooses without being raped. Blaming your actions on her outfit is not going to hold up in any court of law.

The prison system is filled with young Black males who've made bad choices. Rape is one of them. Though estimates say that only one in six of all rapes are reported to the police, do you really want to take your chances?[6] No one that I know wants to be in Kobe Bryant's shoes, accused of rape in Colorado and facing four years to life.

As many as 25% of all women on campus will be victims of rape or attempted rape.[7] Upwards of 80% of these women know and may still see the perpetrator around campus.[8] It often begins with an innocent date or just hanging out with a male friend one night. Things start happening, but he pushes the issue, becoming more insistent and forceful. The outcome can range from attempted sexual assault to rape, and change peoples' lives forever.

Alcohol or drug use by one or both people involved is often another critical factor, so please be careful when you're at the party, club, or drinking with friends.[9] Ladies, travel in groups and look out for one another. Having a drunk male friend walk you home alone after the party is not a wise move. Men, also watch your boys and make sure they're not acting a fool, getting in every woman's face.

Most of all, we have to look out for each other. One of the keys to a successful college experience is to develop a community of trust. Women who are simply trying to unwind with friends at a party shouldn't have to fear for their safety, or deal with hearing "I didn't want to dance with you anyway, bitch." This, along with the many other foul things men say and do around women, is disrespectful and unnecessary. Brothers, we can and must do better. Most importantly, understand that you can not take what you want when it comes at the expense and violation of another person. There's simply no excuse for this.

Change Number Three: We must stop the cycle of drama and foolishness that we put each other through in our relationships.

Do you know why she thinks you're cheating on her? Because the last guy she dealt with cheated. So did the one before that. And that history, combined with your shady, short answers ain't giving her too much confidence in you right now. That's why she's going through your stuff, looking at your cell phone directory, and counting your condoms.

Is this right? Of course not. No woman wants to have to wonder where her man's been, and no man wants to have his wallet searched for phone numbers, especially if he's not doing anything wrong. And what brother wants to be looking over his shoulder, wondering if his girl is looking at him or that other dude across the room? (Yes, you cheat too, ladies, so please don't deny it). Why should anyone have to put up with constant questions and bickering over infidelities, real or imagined? That's a great question. But as long as we continue the current trend of fake-lationships, this is a question that will beg to be answered.

Look at where we are right now. Marriage has become a 50/50 crapshoot. I hear "baby's momma" and "baby's daddy" more than husband and wife. We're laying down and having kids with people that we don't even know. Many times this is because we really don't know ourselves, nor what we want. We hunt for clues in pop-cultural icons, knowing good and well that every other video on BET is centered around strip clubs, bubbly, and pool parties that never went down in my neighborhood. So basically, we've got it all twisted. Our view of relationships can be downright unrealistic and dysfunctional, so going into something with that frame of mind is bound to cause drama.

And that's exactly what we get.

We put ourselves through so much ridiculous nonsense that at some point it just isn't cute anymore. Essentially, we're playing ourselves, and this becomes a cycle that results in unfulfilling experiences at best, and absolute wastes of time at worst. We must create better, healthier, more fulfilling situations. To do this, you first must know and be honest with yourself, and then you need to take your time.

Don't enter a relationship looking for someone to complete you. You're already a whole person, growing and learning daily. Know who you are, what you like, and what you want, then look for someone who you connect with that *compliments* your personality. Sometimes opposites will attract and other times you'll have a lot in common, but what really matters is that you be yourself in the process. Brothers, don't think that now that you're in college you have to be a player. And don't get overconfident and think that you can't get played. Sisters, don't feel like you have to act a certain way or switch your style up. Be comfortable and confident being you, and know the type of people you like to be around and the level of commitment you can make in a relationship. Move at your own pace.

When you're ready to explore relationship possibilities, keep your options open. If you're seeing someone that you don't really know a whole lot about, why would you set up a marriage-type commitment level from the jump? Get to know each other first – and this can't simply be on the physical level if you expect to develop a REAL-lationship. Some of your encounters may just be physically-based, and that is what it is, but both people need to understand that fact. When one person expects more, or is led to believe that there is (or will be) more by the other person's deceptive intentions, that's when feelings get hurt and the drama starts.

I don't see anything wrong with telling someone, "look, I like you, but I'd like to get to know more about you before we commit any further. I also think that we should keep things open and see other people, if that's okay with you." What's wrong with saying that? I'll tell you what's wrong. It's way too honest. Some of you will be okay with the first line – *maybe* – but leave the second line out and do whatever you want to do without telling the other person. Or you'll be sneaky and think that the other person will understand that line two is implicit. Why don't you just open your mouth and say what you want? The worst that can happen is that the other person won't want to see you anymore. No problem. If you're telling them that you want to keep things open, then you're obviously not head-over-heels, so move on.

You'll know when you really like someone. Sometimes it will be early on, sometimes it will slowly evolve. When you get to that point, continue nurturing your relationship and being honest. But until that time, know that all of the games we play with each other eventually come back to us in one way or another.

>> The Three Factors to a Successful Relationship

A relationship can take many forms, especially during college. You may date someone casually, leaving your options open to see other people, or you might have an exclusive commitment to each other. Your relationship might be purely physical, non-sexual, or somewhere in the middle. You may have dated from freshman year through graduation, or your relationship may last all of one night. Whatever the situation or circumstances, there are three basic things that need to be in order for things to work, especially as you move towards the longer-term.

Factor One: The Person

You want to find someone who's excited about who you are, who can make you smile when you've had a bad day. Someone who you can talk openly with. Someone who admires you and makes you feel comfortable and safe. Someone who's attracted to you physically and intellectually. Someone who challenges you with honesty. Someone who can see you with their eyes closed. Someone who you can listen to your favorite CD with and enjoy the melodies of life. Someone who's spontaneous but wise. Someone who glows when you smile. Someone your momma will love and your father will respect. Someone who will care about you the same way that you care about them.

How do you find this special someone? Don't look for them, but keep your eyes open. Don't wait for them, but be patient. Go to the parties and to the clubs, but also join an activity or take a class for fun. It could be someone from your yesterdays or an unknown face from tomorrow. You may be looking at the person right now and not even realize it. Listen to your heart. When it feels right, you'll know.

Factor Two: The Timing

Two people can be the most compatible on paper, get along well, and make hours seem like seconds when they're around each other. They may know everything there is to know about each other and make the perfect theoretical couple, but still not be able to make the relationship magic work, all because of timing.

Many of you may think that I'm talking about a situation when your "perfect, super-special soul mate" is already in a relationship with someone else. That's one example of bad timing. But the timing can also be off when two people are actually in a relationship together.

He wants to commit, but she's afraid because of her last relationship. He's a senior about to graduate while she's a sophomore, worried about what the future holds for them. He wants to make the most of his college years (read: sleep around), but has found "the one" too soon. She's pre-med and trying to buckle down for the MCAT, he has too much time on his hands and needs attention. She's going abroad next semester but just met someone special. She's found a new friend but isn't quite over the last one yet, who still calls a few times a day.

Timing has messed up more than its share of relationships. While many situations can't always be completely blamed on timing, and often can be worked through, timing still is a critical factor. Sometimes it will seem like people come into your life, or re-appear, at just the right time. In other instances when you're facing problems, you'll need to ask yourself, "is this really all about timing?" and then decide what can be done to work things out.

Factor Three: The Communication Lines

In the beginning of a relationship, all you'll want to do is talk and be around each other. You'll be interested in each other's backgrounds, goals, and funny life moments. You'll find yourself discussing favorite movies and childhood memories for hours on end. Relationships that survive and grow will continue this pattern of healthy, substantive communication.

As you develop longer-term relationships you may begin to take things for granted. If you're hanging around with your boyfriend or girlfriend all the time, or even living with them, the special moments that you used to share aren't viewed as all that special any more. Sometimes that "significant" person in your life ends up in the background, caught somewhere in your busy mix of classes and activities.

We need to make time to say and do nice things for our relationship partners. We also need to prioritize simple conversation. Couples who actively engage each other in their various individual pursuits and interests, politics, new personal theories, daily activities, and even campus gossip will be more in tune. Sometimes limited conversation is a clear indicator that you have very little in common with your partner, or that one (or both) of you has changed but left the other in the dark.

No one is going to graduate college as the same person that they were freshman year. If you meet your girlfriend or boyfriend during that first year, and you expect things to last, then you must communicate. If you expect to work through the various challenges that your relationship will face, you need to be open and honest. If you want your relationship to continue moving forward, you have to be willing to talk about your individual wants and needs, in addition to what you want for the relationship. Ideally you will be matched with someone who you look forward to talking with every day, and who you'll continue to vibe with through deep, meaningful conversation. But even in the difficult moments, when you're going through something individually or within the relationship, being able to communicate with your partner will enable the trust and support needed to make your connection last.

At Your Best

> *At your best you are love*
> *You're a positive motivating force within my life*

These lines are from an old Isley Brothers song, later remade by the late Aaliyah. I know some portions of this chapter painted a pretty bleak picture of relationships. There's a lot of work to be done in the relationship game, but this shouldn't take away from the beautiful examples of love around us.

Deep down, we all desire to find someone who warms our souls. When we become comfortable with ourselves and stop playing petty games with each other, we can develop relationships that will last a lifetime. Every couple will have their ups and downs. We all individually have our moody days and make mistakes. When we find someone truly special, they'll understand how we are on our "off days" and will still be there for us. When the relationship itself is the cause of tension, honest communication will be the answer to put things back on track so that you can continue motivating, encouraging, and loving each other.

The What-ifs.

Before I close out this chapter, here are a few assorted relationship questions and answers. For more advice, speak with a mentor, friends, or even your parents. You may not think of mom and dad as the ideal choice for this type of conversation, but they've done everything you have, and always have your best interests in mind. Like I said, relationships can be an extremely confusing time, so when in doubt, talk it out.

- **What if you like someone and don't know how to approach them?** You only live once. Create an opportunity and make your move. Be calm and be yourself. The worst that can happen is that you make a total fool of yourself. But guess what? It happens to us all, so don't let that stop you. (If you do bomb, you'll have a great story to tell later. If you don't, you've got something to do this weekend).

- **What if you want to establish a greater commitment level?** You might want to put some subtle hints out there to see if he or she responds. If that doesn't spark the conversation, then sit down with them and let them know how you feel. Relationships work best when both people are on the same page.

- **What if you meet someone that you'd like better if _____ was different about them?** Please don't take on relationships and make people your personal projects. People don't want to change, especially when they're being forced. There are ways to go about making constructive suggestions once you're in a relationship, but entering into one so that you can put some unsuspecting human being on your "program" is not a sound strategy at all.

- **What if you're seeing someone but meet someone else interesting?** You know what they say about greener grass, right. If you're in a committed relationship, really think about what you want to do before you act. Cheating = imminent drama. Drama eventually gets ugly (slashed tires, keyed cars, nasty notes left on your dorm door, your stuff thrown out of windows, 911, embarrassing arguments in the middle of the cafeteria…You don't want this, do you?)

- **What if you want to break up but fear how your partner will handle it?** Breaking up can also equal imminent drama, but if you're really not into the relationship anymore, fronting and faking is just wasting everyone's time. Don't drag it out because it usually just gets uglier.

- **What if you can't get over him or her?** Everyone goes through periods of heartache. It will be difficult, but try to separate your head from your heart and really assess the situation. If there's a chance things can be worked out, give the other person some time and space then see what happens. If it's over (i.e., they're already in a new relationship or simply don't want to see you anymore), let it go. Your life is bigger than your relationship, so focus on something else. It'll take some time, so stay busy and keep your mind occupied. (You may be tempted to jump into a new relationship right away, or even dig up numbers from your past. This is called "rebounding" and is often looked back upon with the same anguish as a bad hangover).

- **What if you're just not into the whole relationship thing, but all of your friends keep making such a big deal about it?** Get new friends. Just kidding. People operate at their own speed. If your friend's jokes and pressuring bothers you, let them know that they need to settle down. But in the meantime, do what makes you happy. If you're not ready for dating, take your time and move when you want to move.

- **What if you're trying to be in the relationship game, but your time hasn't come yet?** Keep hope alive. It will happen for you. You may want to forgo the club and party scene (where everyone does their hunting), and join a campus activity or spend extra time at the library (where the smart people meet).

- **What if you're having feelings for someone of the same sex?** You may be gay, or exploring your sexuality. College is an emotionally complex time, and homosexuality is rarely an easy topic to address. Seek support at your school LGBT (Lesbian, Gay, Bi-Sexual, Transgender) center, or confide in a close friend or mentor to really explore the issue.

- **What if the person you're seeing says they'll leave you if you don't hurry up and have sex with them?** Show them the door. Why? Because after you give in, what guarantee do you have that they'll call you again?

- **What if the condom breaks?** If you feel it break then take a pit stop and put on a fresh one. (Men, if you ignore it, you're playing with fire...literally). If you find out "after the fact," ladies need to take the morning after pill within 72 hours of having sex (http://www.morningafterpill.org). Both of you should also get tested for STDs ASAP.

- **What if you think you're pregnant?** First, find out for sure, either through a home kit or by visiting Student Health. The longer you delay, the more stress you'll put yourself through. If you are, you're going to have some serious choices to make. Speak with family and close friends for support and counseling. Also seek as much information as possible about your options. If you have a good relationship with the child's father, you can consult with him, but it is my opinion that this decision must ultimately rest with the mother. (If you're not pregnant, you need to read this chapter again because you've obviously missed a few points).

- **What if you think you have an STD?** Go get it confirmed. Don't be embarrassed. You won't be the first person at the clinic with a "burning sensation." There're probably two other people in the waiting room with the same thing. Best to get treatment sooner than later.

- **What if you haven't been checked for any STDs in a while, but you've been sexually active?** Go see the doctor. Even if you've used condoms, it's best to know for sure. Many STDs don't have any significant initial signs, so if you have an active sex life, especially with multiple partners, you should get checked at least twice a year.

- **What if you're in a monogamous relationship and she's on the birth control pill – do you still need to use a condom?** Yes. Just because *you're* in a monogamous relationship doesn't mean that your partner is in one.

- **What if you have a question that wasn't asked?** Ask it online at www.lionsstory.org/college. We'll try to answer as many as we can and post them to the website. Some will be printed in future editions of the book.

PART FOUR: CHALLENGES, CHOICES, AND REWARDS

EIGHTEEN. STARTING RIGHT

The importance of your college freshman year can not be understated. Yes, it's a lot of pressure. It may even be unfair. I remember a conversation I had with a college friend a few years after we had graduated. Looking back, we both wondered how we made it through those first few semesters. Most of the people we knew (ourselves included) weren't prepared socially or academically for such a challenge. We thought we knew everything, but most of us could only cook one meal, noodles and sauce (we called it "spaghetti," but it was really just boiled noodles and sauce straight out of the jar). We knew very little about the world outside of our neighborhoods, and we had absolutely no idea what real studying was.

Entering college as the "new kids on the block" may intimidate you a little bit, and may even cause you to second-guess a few things. Whatever you do, don't second-guess yourself! Instead, take a close look at what you're doing to prepare for the start of your college career and the beginning of each ensuing semester. You have the talent to succeed. The real question is whether you'll properly position yourself to take advantage of your talent. The answer is in how you prepare.

A proper introduction

High schoolers receive a heap of mail when being courted by colleges, and a brand new stack after being accepted. The school you choose to attend will send you housing and activities packets, financial aid information, and maybe a half-dozen welcome letters from different departments on campus. Among this pile of envelopes will probably be some information detailing various orientation and freshman-specific programs. Read this material thoroughly, as these will be your first tickets to success.

Each college runs their orientations differently. Some will offer programs for students to attend in the summer, prior to the official start of the school year. Others will bundle a variety of workshops and programs into the move-in period or first few weeks of school when student's schedules are lighter. Some will offer freshman courses during the year that serve as an introduction to different aspects of college life. Some schools will have a combination of these options.

Find out what orientation programs your school sponsors and be sure to participate. Don't blow them off, and don't go with the attitude that you already know this stuff and don't need to be there. Some orientations will start out slow and cover some pretty basic information. Chemistry 101 starts out the same way – the periodic table, H_2O, yada yada yada. Next thing you know, you've got a problem set that's giving you trouble on question number one. Orientation workshops will eventually get into the nuances of college life and break down how you should prepare, which resources are available to you, and which people on campus you should get in your corner. Summer pre-college programs and freshman seminars will give you valuable classroom experience, possibly in a more nurturing environment. Go into these programs knowing that you're making an investment in your college career, then soak up as much information as possible.

What's the big deal?

What's so crucial about getting a good start in college? The numbers don't lie, so let's look at two examples that will break things down.

Example 1: You take 8 classes your freshman year (4 each semester). You get four "A's", two "A-minuses", a "B-plus", and a "B." This gives you a cumulative GPA of 3.7. Excellent work! Now suppose you take 8 more classes sophomore year, but this time you get all "B's." Your sophomore year GPA will be a 3.0, but your overall GPA will be a 3.35. If you get "B's" through the rest of your junior and senior years (16 more classes), your cumulative GPA will end up being a 3.17. And this is all due to only one good year. Imagine what can be done with a healthy mix of "A's" and "B's" during your final three years. You'll be in the 3.5 range, which is a good place to be.

Example 2: Again you take 8 classes freshman year. You get three "D's", three "C's", a "B-minus" and an "A." Your GPA for the year is 1.96. Ouch. Welcome to academic probation. For your 8 sophomore year classes, you study with our friend from Example 1 and get all "B's." Your semester GPA is a 3.0, but your cumulative is a 2.48. That's an improvement, but it's between a "C-plus" and a "B-minus" average. Suppose you also get all "B's" for the rest of your college career. Your overall GPA will be 2.74. This is not the end of the world, but look at what one poor year did to three average ones.

The moral of this story is: don't dig a hole for yourself, because it's extremely tough to climb out. Even if you end up being an average "B" student the rest of the way, you'll still never see a "B" cumulative because of that hole. What if you get a super shovel senior year and have a straight "A" semester? It'll boost your cumulative GPA a bit more, but prospective grad schools and future employers will probably only see your grades up through junior year. Hey, it's a great moral victory and a good personal accomplishment, but it's always best to show your good foot sooner, not later.

Instead of digging a ditch, build a cushion. Strive to maintain that cushion, but know that if you have an average or even a bad semester, your cumulative won't suffer drastically. This will also help you preserve a positive attitude and a healthy level of self-confidence. Having to struggle out of a hole can lead to excess pressure, doubt, and detachment from school. On the flipside, academic success is the breeding ground for even more success.

How do you get this cushion? Well, if you've been paying attention since page one, then you should already have a good idea. To get started, you must first establish the cushion (or high GPA) as your goal, and understand how important it is to do well early. Don't stress over it or put too much added pressure on yourself. Simply believe that you can reach your goal, then closely follow the Formula for Success, using all of the resources available to you.

Summary

Many people like to think that each semester they start out with a blank grade sheet. A clean slate. A new opportunity. This is partially true, because each term is a chance to take new classes and earn new grades. But instead of starting with all zeroes, or an empty grade sheet, begin each semester with the mind state that you have a 4.0, and it's up to you to keep it. In other words, start at perfection then try to maintain it. If you expect to earn an "A," and believe that it is already yours, you will focus your efforts and approach the class more seriously than if you have no expectations or simply want to get whatever grade you end up with. How you start is how you'll finish. If you want an "A" you can't wait until the final exam to start working for it.

Near the beginning of each semester it's also important that you revisit your overall academic goals, study strategies, and performance from the previous term. What could you have done differently? What do you want to accomplish this time around? Re-read portions of this book, spend time with your journal, and make sure you begin each semester feeling refreshed, motivated, and excited about another opportunity to succeed.

NINETEEN. A MAJOR DECISION

Let's start with a little secret. *It may not matter what you choose to major in.* I know business students who went on to medical school, and pre-meds with MBAs. I know people who studied everything under the sun, from psychology and economics to English and Spanish, and ended up in the tech industry. I also know engineers who've gone on to law school, and others who write books.

Why am I telling you this? So that you can finally settle on that ceramics major and move on with your life? Only if you really have a passion for pottery. Jokes aside, my real intent here is to ease the stress of choosing your major. Some people will tell you that this is the most important decision you can make, even more important than selecting a school, and that your entire future rides on this choice. Today, this simply isn't true.

A generation or two ago, people picked a major, got a job in their field of study, and made a 30-plus year career out of it. Teachers taught, accountants crunched numbers, and doctors saw patients until it was time to collect their retirement. Times have changed, and this isn't your grandfather's career track.

College graduates no longer stay locked into one job their entire life. While bouncing around to different gigs used to be frowned upon as a sign of instability, in today's job market, it may be a matter of necessity. You may not be able to locate your ideal job immediately after graduation and need to take on something temporary to pay the bills. Or you may in fact land an ideal situation, only to have your company be bought out by another firm and down-sized, wiping your job from the books. These instances, along with job dissatisfaction, geographic or life-changes, and the desire to do something different have triggered many grads to explore other options in their field or move to another career path all together.

Know what's out there

One of the first things you want to do when you're seriously contemplating your major is to scope out the terrain. As an exercise, take out a sheet of paper and write down all of the jobs and careers that you can think of in five minutes. Okay, it's an exercise, so that means you should actually do it. I'll wait.

Did you do it? Did you struggle to come up with a large list? It shouldn't be a surprise. We grow up wanting to be doctors and policemen, then we hear that lawyers make more than cops and don't get shot at, so we edit our list. We see the TV anchor person or the big-time actress and pay little attention to the other hundreds of names in the credits who make these things possible. Every kid shooting hoops in the neighborhood wants to play in the NBA. They've never given any thought to owning the team. And because they already know they're going to the NBA, they're not paying attention at their high school "Career Day" when the doctor and lawyer visit, along with the cop making one final plea.

How can you decide what you want to do if you don't even know what the choices are? Spend some time with a career book and on the internet browsing the different options. If you have a wide field of interest, look at the different occupations that are related. Also look at other areas for things that catch your interest or have ties to something that you want to do. Many jobs require a wide range of skills and backgrounds, and may combine more than one of your interests, giving you a "best of both worlds" effect.

The right fit

If you choose a particular major but then dread all of the courses you're taking for that major, then something's not right. If you picked a major based on projected income only, and have no desire to actually work in that field, how exactly do you plan to earn that income?

What do you like to do? As another exercise, think about that question and make a list. Jot down anything that comes to mind, even things that you enjoy but haven't done in a while, or things that you think you'll like but haven't been able to try yet.

Now think about what you want to do – what kind of job can you see yourself in? Where do you want to be in five years? Write down your thoughts. Now look at your two lists. Is there any overlap between what you like and what you want to do? Why or why not? Is your "what you want to do" list based on external factors – money, job availability, parental/other wishes? Are you settling for what comes easy to you or what you think you'd be good at? Are you afraid to really push yourself or step out in a risky (read: artsy, non-traditional, entrepreneurial) career track?

Stepping stones and part-time seeds

We often play it safe, especially when it comes to major decisions. Maybe you have a certain path that you dream of taking, but your intuition tells you to move with the back up plan. As a brother with bills to pay and mouths to feed, I truly understand the need for a steady income. For some of you, your major may be a means to a completely different end. My technology background netted me a nice full-time job, but my passions are in education and writing, which I do on the side. Fortunately, I've also used my technology experience in those pursuits, streamlining my website operations and facilitating a lot of business and administrative functions through the internet.

You may go through an assortment of experiences which all provide valuable lessons and help you put together your big picture. Once you key in on what you want to do, there will be a variety of paths you can take to get there.

Write your own ticket

Don't be afraid to go against the grain and create a career path that truly fits your dreams. Revisit your "what you like to do" list and really think of ways that you can get paid to do what you enjoy or what really interests you, rather than settling for something less desirable. Even in a tough job market, there's always room for ingenuity and new ideas. Furthermore, if you really explore the possibilities, the job you want may already be out there.

Suppose you have an interest in medicine, but also enjoy traveling. You may be able to do medical research in a foreign country. If you're a talented writer, you can write for a medical journal or website, or work on your own book. If you have an interest in education, you can teach the sciences on a variety of grade levels, or work for an educational non-profit and specialize in pre-med preparation.

The opportunities are out there, but if you don't see them, you can create them yourself. Launching your own company is nothing more than paying a few licensing fees and submitting your paperwork. You could design websites and make your own company's site look so good that people will think you've got a full-time staff ten people deep. Don't limit yourself and your dreams. Be passionate about finding your passion. When you're doing something that you enjoy, your overall experience is that much more enjoyable.

Summary: What, how, and when

Much of this chapter talked about possibilities after college, because essentially, this is what a major is preparing you for. Think about some of the things that you enjoy or are interested in, then work on identifying options that will be a good fit. After you explore all of the requirements and details, you should have a good idea of a major that will work for you.

If you have a few different interests, you may want to see if there's a major that would be useful across the board, or if there's a way that you can tie things together. Or you may want to make sure that your major, and the electives that you take outside of your major, cover a wide range of topics. This way you'll have a broader background and will be exposed to more information that can possibly help you later.

Many campuses have a career counseling center and host a variety of career workshops. Take advantage of these opportunities, but also create your own. Talk to professors in your areas of interest, or reach out to other people who are currently working in the field you'd like to pursue. Join campus organizations and pre-professional societies, go to conferences, and network whenever possible. Look at career websites and stay informed about new opportunities.

The sooner that you can identify something that interests you, the better you can position yourself. Spend some time with the decision, but know that what you choose today may not be the career that you end up in, nor be your major next year. Sixty-percent of all college students change their major.[1] Doing so late in the game may require you to extend your stay in school, but if you're really unhappy in your major and believe that the change will benefit you, it's better to spend the extra time than getting a degree in something that you don't really want to do.

TWENTY. ADDITIONAL ACADEMIC OPTIONS

This chapter covers a few more issues you may encounter in school, either by choice or circumstance.

Studying abroad and other travel opportunities

Travel is one of the best ways to not only gain insight into how the world works, but also develop a greater self-perspective. Studying abroad offers the opportunity for students to immerse themselves in a particular culture for a semester, while taking courses and continuing their degree work. Students do not necessarily need to be proficient in a foreign language and can typically apply financial aid towards a study abroad program. While I personally did not study abroad due to my rigorous engineering schedule, I know students who've studied in places such as Ghana, Spain, London, the Dominican Republic, Japan, and more. They all treasured the experience and strongly recommended it to others, so look into the opportunities at your school.

Most students who study abroad do so in either their sophomore or junior year, so if you think this is something you'd like to pursue, put it in your 4-year plan. Be advised that the spots are often limited and competition can be stiff, so keep your grades tight to make the best impression possible.

If you're not able to study abroad, or are unsure about spending a whole semester away, look into a summer travel program. There are a variety of options to choose from, some which may give college credit, others which offer employment opportunities, and some which are training seminars for a wide range of topics. Check with your school's study abroad office for starters, and also search online.

Finally, for a short trip, take advantage of academic and organizational conferences which occur throughout the year. These offer excellent opportunities to network, gain valuable information, and experience a different part of the country. Often your school or organization will assist with your travel expenses, or even fully sponsor your trip.

178 The African American Student's Guide to Excellence in College

Choosing a minor, dual-major, or customized program

Occasionally students will have a unique academic interest that the pre-defined list of majors does not satisfy. Usually this challenge can be solved, but the exact method depends on the options available at your school.

Some schools offer **dual-degrees** where a student may pursue two undergraduate degrees at the same time. The Management and Technology program, combining business and engineering, was a popular choice at Penn. Another possibility is **submatriculation**, where students are accepted into a Masters degree program while in undergrad. Students will begin taking graduate courses in their latter years of undergrad, then finish up the graduate degree usually in an additional year. Typically dual-degree and submatriculation options take five years to complete.

Another option is to **create your own major**. To get started, you will have to consult with an academic advisor or department head about a specific course itinerary and degree requirements. Some schools may not make this option known, but still may be open to your suggestions, so if you have something in mind, speak to your advisor.

Finally, we have a **minor**. You may know you want to major in Electrical Engineering but also have an interest in Spanish. In this case, by confirming your intentions with your academic advisor, you can then plan on taking a series of Spanish courses over your four years of school and earn a minor. Your advisor or your school academic publications will explain the process, along with the minimum number of classes you'll need to qualify for a minor.

Transferring schools

Students elect to transfer to a different school for a variety of reasons – not fitting in socially, not being challenged academically, not being in the ideal financial situation, moving closer to home, switching from a 2-year to a 4-year school, moving to a smaller school, and more.

If you're considering transferring, take the school selection process seriously. You're essentially shopping for the right fit all over again. Since you've spent some time in school you should have a clearer picture of what will work and what won't. Make sure that your new school will successfully meet your needs. Also be certain to handle all of the appropriate logistics so that your credits transfer with you.

Time off

Not everyone's academic career will be four years of smooth sailing. Some of you may have to put things on pause for financial reasons, academic reasons, or other personal issues. Taking a break from school is not the end of the world. In some cases it's actually a benefit because it allows you to refocus and essentially make a new start. This is especially helpful if you weren't doing as well as possible the first time around.

Before leaving school, speak to your advisor, financial aid, campus housing, and any other relevant people so that any paperwork and details are handled. You don't want to be billed for anything by mistake, or have any other loose ends.

Set a timetable for your return. Do you need a semester off? A year? Longer? Even if you don't have a clear picture, try to develop a rough estimate. You don't want to leave things wide open and lose sight of completing your degree.

Finally, just because you're not in school during your time off doesn't mean that you have to stop learning. Consider taking a non-credit course at a local community college or developing your own personal study routine. If you can use your time off to get a jump on things, that may provide the boost you need when it's time to return to campus.

Returning to school

It's natural to feel a bit out of place when you come back to school, especially if it's been a while. For some students, their return to school may be after years of working, marriage, kids, and a whole life of experiences. Others may come back after only a semester away. In either case, *return with a purpose*.

Know what you want to get out of your experiences and be sure to make the most of your second chance. Some of you may want to focus purely on the books this go around, and that's fine. But you may also consider getting involved in at least one activity, especially one connected to your major or field of interest. Even if you're an older returning student, as a part of the student body you have the same privileges as everyone else. Younger students can benefit from your experiences, so don't be deterred from getting involved.

An extra semester (or two)

Graduating in five years instead of four is becoming more commonplace for a variety of reasons. The most important thing is that you graduate. If you anticipate needing extra time, you can create a financial plan that will get the school bills paid and stretch out your academic program to take pressure off of yourself. For many students, myself included, this was a smart move.

Summary

During college, you will be required to make numerous decisions which will affect your overall academic experience. Know what your options are and choose the best fit. Don't be afraid to challenge yourself (studying abroad, customizing a major) and don't shy away from difficult choices (taking time off, transferring, returning to school).

TWENTY-ONE. PERSONAL FINANCE AND PAYING FOR SCHOOL

Why is money such an important topic in college? For starters, money, or more accurately, a lack of it, is one of the top reasons why students don't return to school. Secondly, if you think about it, you're entering into an important phase of life. Being broke can and will limit your options. Contrary to the popular belief that most students are a work-study paycheck away from poverty, you actually can put away some savings, pay your school bill, and even have a little spending cash if you make a plan. Read on…

Managing your money

The first step in managing money is to **get money**. You're in college to learn and prepare for your future, but this doesn't mean that you can't also work and build your finances. Many students will get a work-study job on campus and do full-time summer work at an internship, department store, restaurant, or other job. Some students may be going to school part-time and working full-time. Others don't get an official job, but have a side hustle such as braiding or cutting hair, DJing parties, or building websites. Choose the right scenario to fit your schedule and your needs. See Chapter 15 for more information. If you are working, sign up for direct deposit. This will save you from wasting time in a bank line, and help you fight the urge to spend all of your money.

Getting a job is not the only way to bring money in. Look for **additional opportunities** to generate some easy cash. Many research universities will have various experiments and studies that will pay you for participating. Weigh these options carefully; some may be dangerous or not worth the time involved. There are many other ways that you can make money such as selling goods on Ebay or submitting something to a poetry, essay, or photography contest, and more. Get creative and brainstorm other outlets.

The next step is to **minimize expenses**. What are you currently paying for that you can get for free, cut down on, replace with a cheaper product, or eliminate all together? Cash not spent is cash available, so analyze your spending habits and develop a budget.

Here's an example of some of the things you can factor in: If you buy a lot of CDs and don't listen to them, consider starting a CD pool with some friends to cut costs, check out the various free internet radio stations, or download your favorite songs (of course, I'm referring to legal downloading). If you eat out a lot, plan on cutting back, especially if you've already paid for an on-campus meal plan. If you're thinking about living off campus, try to find a place that bundles in your utility costs for a flat rate, or make sure you do whatever you can to keep the bills low (i.e., don't run the AC all night). If you really don't need it, consider leaving your car at home, or even selling it.

These are just a few ideas to get you thinking. The important thing is to make sure that you take your spending and cost-cutting seriously and look for ways to save money instead of spending it blindly. To go with that point, we all need to **eliminate the term "disposable income"** from our vocabularies. Disposable means "throw away." Who tosses money in the trash? It's cool to enjoy yourselves every now and then, or even occasionally splurge on something you really want or need, but anytime you spend money, do it with a purpose in mind (education, entertainment, travel, personal needs, etc). If it's a waste, don't buy it.

As a college student, you must also fight the credit card temptation and **avoid debt**. You'll already probably have a nice sized student loan, so why add on to your debt with back-breaking credit card interest rates. Paying the minimum each month isn't going to do you any good, as the bill will just keep growing.

Credit cards aren't necessarily a bad thing, but you have to use them responsibly. You don't need one for every store you've ever been to. Two non-store specific cards (i.e., Visa, Mastercard, Discover, etc) are fine. One should be a debit card, which is tied directly to your checking account. This takes the money out of your account as you spend it, and is ideal for small purchases. When you need to put something major on your credit card, like school books or a spring break trip, have a plan for paying the bill off in large chunks. This will save you a lot of cash and headaches in the long run.

Next, learn to take advantage of the best kind of money around – **other people's money**. Don't let important holidays pass by without getting what you need. When your parents ask you what you want, don't say "whatever." Have your list ready, or just get the cash. If your parents are helping you with your school bills, car note, or other expenses, that's a beautiful thing. Don't ever take that for granted, but instead, really think about how much money they're actually saving you, then make sure to use that money wisely. Which brings us to the final point...

Establish a personal savings plan. Whenever you get a paycheck or come up on some cash, pay yourself first. Don't spend it and don't pay any bills until you've put some of it away in your savings account. Many of us live check to check because our mindset isn't focused on wealth. We want to spend everything now on things to impress other people instead of putting money away to prepare for the future. If you're ever going to start your own business and/or have a family, you need to start saving for these things now. Create a savings goal and a plan to achieve it. As you begin to accumulate a nice sum of cash, look into different interest-earning options so that your money can create more money for you.

Financing your education

Paying for school is not an easy task, especially when you factor in the rising costs and the miscellaneous expenses that you'll incur (books, living costs, etc). As we've discussed throughout the book, you need to map out a strategy for how to succeed in school. You'll need an additional plan that details how you'll pay for it.

Before you enter college you should give some serious thought to paying the bill. You'll receive a lot of loan and financial aid information. Read through this carefully, and if anything doesn't make sense, contact the school or speak with an independent financial advisor who has experience in school tuition payment plans. You can also find information online or via the many scholarship reference books available at your local bookstore or library.

Even with a solid advance plan, many students will still struggle with paying their school bill. Let's revisit some of the items discussed in the previous section and apply them specifically to this situation.

First, nothing ever beats other people's money, or in this case, **scholarships**. Do an extensive search of all scholarships available – those specific to your college, national and international awards, etc. For some starting points, visit our website, www.lionsstory.org/college. There are literally hundreds upon hundreds of sources available. Don't sleep on the small scholarships – the $100, $250, and $500 awards. That's money you didn't have before. Also, put your time into the scholarship process. Make sure your paperwork is thorough, neat, and complete, and that you meet the application deadline. Keep copies of the materials you submit in case you can re-use them for another scholarship. The search and application process takes time, but if you half-do it, then that's just time wasted.

The other good thing about scholarships, besides the money, is that they'll keep you on your toes academically. Many scholarships have a minimum GPA requirement to apply. Some scholarships will renew each year if you maintain that GPA. So not only are you getting free money, but you have built-in extra incentive to do well.

The next thing you want to look at is **minimizing school bill expenses**. Some students work in the dining hall or at a local restaurant so they can eat for free. Others will become a Resident Advisor or similar position for free rent. These moves can save you thousands in living expenses. See what options are available at your school.

Another way to potentially cut down on the school bill is to stay in close contact with your financial aid advisor. If you have a change in your financial situation, let them know and see what they can do for you. If at any point the numbers don't look right, have them reevaluate your package. There've been many students who can safely call the financial aid office a home away from home, but if that's what it takes, then be persistent and make your case. Also talk to other advisors, mentors, college graduates, faculty and staff, and anyone else who may be able to provide you with information about financial help. *Don't let money keep you away from your degree.*

An additional cost-cutting technique is to get out as soon as possible. If you're really motivated, you can actually plan to graduate a year or a semester early. Many students end up spending additional time in school due to a lack of focus, a poor start, or because they changed their major. This extra time not only adds to your school bill, but also defers your ability to earn a decent college graduate's salary. Many freshmen aren't even thinking about these types of issues, but you need to before you end up having to scramble to pay for a few wasted semesters.

Finally, explore **alternate routes** to finishing school. One of the best kept secrets is that many schools offer tuition benefits for full-time employees. This means that if you work at your school in a salaried position (i.e., not a work-study job), they'll give you a paycheck plus pay your tuition. Some schools will even pay a certain percentage of your tuition at another school. The drawback to this is that you'll have to go to school part-time, because most tuition benefits will only pay for a couple of classes per semester. Nevertheless, it's a good opportunity to earn some money plus continue working towards your degree. I know students who have successfully employed this technique to finish undergraduate and others who did their graduate work this way. I earned my Masters degree through a tuition benefit program. Similarly, many companies will finance employee's graduate and professional degrees, while the military also offers a variety of tuition assistance programs for undergraduate and advanced degrees, so look into these possibilities and make them work for you.

Summary

Take your money seriously in school. If you plan to save instead of struggle, then that will be your outcome. If you explore all of the available financial resources and opportunities then follow through on each, financial issues should not be an impediment to your graduation.

TWENTY-TWO. THE COLOR LINE

W.E.B. Du Bois' often-quoted declaration that the problem of the twentieth century would be the "color line" was, and still is right on the money. Racism is perhaps the truest testament to the cruel frailty of human nature. The society that we know today, built upon the not-so-distant realities of chattel slavery, is the by-product of centuries of racist practices. Embedded within our world's inner-workings are institutionalized examples of racism, still alive and kicking. Your collegiate career will undoubtedly provide demonstrations of racism in action.

Staring in its face

Racism fundamentally stems from a fear of difference, a lack of understanding, and an utter disregard for the rights of others. It's a prime example of the "us" vs. "them" mentality. Whenever people are able to create a "them" category, the doors open for prejudice, exploitation, and violence. Fortunately, on most college campuses, severe issues of racial intolerance are not as prevalent as in the past. The overall climate in this country has become more accepting of cultural differences, such that the wide-spread sit-ins and boycotts of the 1960's are no longer required. However, this does not mean that the work is done or that incidents don't still occur nationwide.

Many of your experiences with racism may be more subtle – a questionable remark from a professor, or white students not valuing your presence in class. As discussed earlier, prevailing attitudes about race may generate inner confusion about your talents and skills. One of the greatest dangers of racism is its ability to further victimize the victim. Whether you experience an overt racist act or do not feel like you're a true part of the school environment due to race, it's essential that you draw strength in affirming your presence. It's natural to question ourselves, but by learning to rephrase the questions, you can empower yourself to look at things from a wider perspective. The next section offers an example of "reframing the questions."

Self-segregation

How many times is a white college student asked why she decided to join a predominantly white sorority or select all white roommates? Has anyone ever wondered why all of the white kids are sitting together in the cafeteria?

Whenever the question of African American self-segregation comes up, this is always my first response. Why is it that when a Black student on a majority white campus chooses to spend an hour at lunch with friends, who also happen to be African American, these students are doing something offensive or questionable to the majority culture? Why is joining an African American organization to celebrate and learn more about your culture considered a separatist act? Why are students of color questioned when they choose to stick together? What about white students and their social clubs? And frankly, why are we so concerned about any of this?

The answer lies in the fact that students of color on majority white campuses represent "diversity" to the majority culture. While this statement is an undisputable fact, it is also 100% Eurocentric. It treats you, the African American student, as an object, instead of a self-empowered individual with your own intentions and ideals.

Perhaps you could care less about diversifying someone else's environment and selected a particular college to explore your own cultural identity, or simply because you liked what the school had to offer. Further, what is often lost in this discussion is the fact that by being members of a predominantly white institution, African American students are automatically and implicitly a part of the wider campus culture. No Black student at a predominantly white school will be taking all Black courses taught by an all Black faculty roster. For the most part, African American students will be immersed in the same collegiate culture that Asian, Latino, and white students experience. Whatever social time students opt to spend among peers of the same racial background is minimal in the larger scheme, and further, is their business.

Summary: The ways of the world

For better or for worse, segregation is still a salient feature of society at large. Funny that no one seems to wonder why *all* of the lunch tables at many urban public schools have Black students sitting there, or why academic achievement can still be clearly measured in black and white. Returning to W.E.B. Du Bois, while he's best known as a supporter of integration, his latter stance was one of "organized and deliberate" self-segregation for Blacks to benefit themselves.[1] In my view, this translates to proactive thought and action.

Instead of being "stuck" in the 'hood, can our proximity be taken advantage of and our resources pooled to gain ownership of our communities and guide our futures? Can our African American organizations on campus, living-learning programs, Africana studies departments, and coalitions of students, staff, and faculty be forces of collaboration to create academic, cultural, economic, and social enrichment programs for the benefit of all? You can call this self-segregation. You can also call it common sense. If African Americans don't take up our own cause, who will?

America was founded upon a concept of democracy that did not include us, but the current reality in this country is one of diversity in which our contributions cannot be denied. Eurocentric cultural ideals continue to take center stage, but the overall identity of America has unquestionably been shaped by all of its people, for true diversity does not deny differences. It is imperative that African Americans continue to enhance their understanding of their past and their culture, and proudly celebrate it. It is equally important that we continue to successfully navigate the color line, and make our place in the multi-cultural world around us.

Many of our work and life experiences will occur in richly diverse environments, so we must not ignore this reality while in college. This means that you should be active in campus-wide organizations and events, study with students of other cultures, critically engage professors, and utilize your full student privilege. Don't limit your experiences for any reason, but become an active participant to fulfill your needs, not to be an object of diversity. Do not compromise your cultural integrity or your desire to develop your cultural identity. Your college experience – a small but significant piece of your life journey – is about *you*. Understanding that fact will provide strength and resilience in the face of racism.

TWENTY-THREE.
GRADUATION: WALKING TALL

This is what it's all about. Finally, after years of courses and questions, struggles and stress, you get to don the cap and gown and be part of the ceremony that marks the completion of your collegiate career. Your graduation is one of life's important markers, and a moment that you'll look back on for years to come. It's not only a special time for you, but also for your family and friends. This is why I chose to include this chapter in the book.

I didn't participate in my undergraduate graduation ceremonies. Though my school's guidelines would have permitted me to attend, I still had an additional semester of classes ahead of me and I didn't want to go through the motions of finishing school if I wasn't truly finished. A few years later when I looked back on my decision, I regretted it because I realized that my logic was extremely self-centered and stubborn.

Fortunately, I was given another opportunity, when I earned my Master's degree. That time around I made sure I was a part of the big show because I understood that it wasn't just about me. My graduation represented a culmination of personal and family achievements and sacrifices, and was a tremendous moment of pride for my parents, brother, grandparents, God mothers, and extended family and friends. It would be unfair for me to deny them this special occasion. As someone who has since attended many graduations of friends and family members, and witnessed the tears of joy and accomplishment, I now understand this even more. And as a parent, I can't even begin to imagine how emotional it will be to see my children receive their degrees when their time comes.

Pay attention to details

When I graduated, we had to fill out some paperwork and make fitting appointments for the cap and gown, so when graduation time rolls around for you, make sure to read all of those mailings, flyers, and e-mails, and take note of the various deadlines. It's going to be a busy time for you (when isn't?), but don't let your graduation responsibilities slip by.

Summary: Never walking alone

You may have had to stay for an extra year or two of college, or taken time off and returned later, and are unable to walk in a graduation ceremony with the close friends and classmates who you began your college career with. If possible, support them when their time comes to graduate, and hopefully some of them will return once you finish. Either way, nothing can take away the many memories that you shared, going back to freshman year. Think about those special moments during your graduation ceremony.

You may have lost someone important to you – a family member or close friend – or not have a strong connection to your family right now. You may feel like you'll be alone when you graduate, and will have no one to share it with. You won't be alone, however. You'll be surrounded by hundreds or thousands of classmates, many whose faces you've never noticed before, but are all wearing the same glow as yours. You will truly feel a sense of connection to them, perhaps for the very first time. And the spirit of our ancestors - from those family members who were close to us, to the many unknown names and faces who sacrificed so much so that you could be where you are - that spirit will also be with you, celebrating in your achievement.

African Americans have struggled relentlessly and continue to face numerous daunting obstacles. We owe it to ourselves to celebrate each and every beautiful moment possible. Graduation is one such time, and each graduate adds their own bit of glow to our collective brilliance.

TWENTY-FOUR. WHAT'S NEXT?

As a college graduate, you'll have a wide range of options to consider. Do you want to go to grad school right away or first work for a while? Should you return home to save up some money or stay on your own? Are you prepared to move across the country or have you gotten used to your college city? Should you do a post-bac program? Can you afford to travel before starting your career? Are you ready for life's next transitional phase?

Hopefully the answer to the last question is "yes," because your post-college preparation must begin long before you have your degree in hand. What you do from the first day of school will have an effect on what you're able to do after you graduate. Just as with other stages of your life, college and post-college are closely connected. Making the right decisions in college will help position you for a variety of lucrative post-college possibilities.

Throughout the text I've attempted to make this connection by not simply focusing on immediate goals, but encouraging you to always keep the bigger picture in mind. The points below will synthesize some of the information previously discussed, and introduce a few new topics.

- **Make your ticket shine.** Your grades, your activities, and your accomplishments are your ticket to the future. Excel academically, get involved on campus, and be the type of person that people want to have on their team. These things are all within your control. Take care of your business and you'll have a wide range of offers and opportunities to choose from.

- **Identify a purpose early.** The difference between how a successful pre-med student studies organic chemistry and how an undeclared major prepares for a random free elective is like night and day. When you know that your coursework satisfies a future objective and is taking you closer to where you want to be, you'll push harder and work with much more intensity.

When you don't know why you're doing something, those "why bother" moments can trigger days of procrastination.

- **The importance of networking.** I self-published my first novel and happened to send a copy of it to an editor I met at a book conference. She passed it on to another editor friend of hers, and two phone calls later I had a book deal with Random House. A few months after the book was re-launched, I reconnected with a college friend who was also working on a book through Random House. We met for lunch and I was offered a freelance writing job at Okayplayer.com, which happened to be the website for some of my favorite music artists. This is the power of networking – I didn't submit one book proposal or résumé. Yeah, I was lucky to be in the right place, having the right conversations, but that's really all that networking is.

- **Dare to be different.** If the corporate route isn't for you, find something that is. Or if no one from your block has gone on to a suit and tie position, don't let that deter you from your Wall Street dreams.

- **It's okay return to the nest.** I know most of you probably don't want to go back to your old bedroom at your parent's house now that you have your degree, but sometimes it's better to take the free rent and make a solid plan than over-paying for a dumpy apartment while you wait on something to happen.

- **Give back.** As an alum, think about the other students who can benefit from your knowledge, connections, and experiences. Find ways to stay in touch with them either through a student organization, alumni association, or other means. Even things as simple as alumni-student e-mail mentoring can provide students with direction and real world stories. Also, if you feel a connection to your school or a particular department, consider making a financial donation.

- **Go back.** If you're able, reunite with old friends and classmates during your school's homecoming festivities. This is a great way to maintain friendships and stay connected to your school.

- **Finish the race.** It's your final semester of school and it's starting to get sunny outside. You've got your job or grad school choice lined up. What's to stop you from taking the rest of the semester off and enjoying yourself? After all, you put in three and a half years of quality work, right? That's a solid case, and a tough one to argue, because even the best students will be tempted to take it easier. But it's important to finish what you've started. You've come this far, and the end is right around the corner, so push through until the race is done.

TWENTY-FIVE. THE ACADEMIC VILLAGE: NOTES FOR FACULTY, ADMINISTRATORS, AND PARENTS

My colleague and mentor, Dr. Howard Stevenson, incorporates the African-centered theme "It takes a village to raise a child" into many aspects of his work. During his time as Faculty Master of W.E.B. Du Bois College House on Penn's campus, he extended the concept by posing the critical question, "what does it take to create the village?" In order to truly provide for our students and ensure their positive development, this is a question that we must address.

The success of African American college students depends on a strong, purposeful support system. Some students will display a natural ability to effectively navigate the challenges and changes that college life introduces, with little or no outside intervention. Others, even students who have achieved tremendous success in high school, will struggle with the academic and social adjustments necessary. Without a system of checks and balances, students may be left to suffer silently on their own, often resulting in academic probation, social anxieties, depression, or another drop-out statistic.

Students may select an HBCU or a smaller institution due to their commitment to providing greater comprehensive support. Larger schools may also provide resources such as mentoring and living-learning programs. In either case, for these retention programs to be successful, they must be monitored and assessed. Are students using them? Do they meet students' needs? Are they having an effect on retention rates? Are GPAs rising? Do students have a better overall experience? Are more African American high school students interested in applying to a particular school due to the engaging and encouraging atmosphere created on campus?

Positive results in these and other areas are the building blocks of a true *academic village*. This reality is possible if it is designated as an objective and prioritized accordingly. We all are essential players in making this village concept work. The following are some suggestions that can be employed:

Two R's, not one

Many schools will focus on recruiting but pay little attention to retention. These two functions must work hand-in-hand. Don't entice students with the promise of opportunities then fail to provide the support they'll need. Students may need to be shown how to take advantage of the available resources and apply themselves, instead of given a handout listing various office locations and website links.

Many African American students have never truly swum before, and college life can often resemble the deep end. Systems must be in place to provide assistance. *Colleges and universities must be committed to the retention of their students and must demonstrate this commitment through a purposeful, multi-faceted program.* This program must take into consideration the specific needs created by cultural differences (learning styles, prior educational experiences, cultural understanding, etc).

Layers of managed mentoring

Mentoring is a simple approach to providing support and encouragement. Many schools offer some form of mentoring. I advise a multi-dimensional approach, facilitated by a central office (Academic Support Services, Minority Programs) or managed by a mentoring advisory board comprised of at least one faculty member, one staff member, and two students (possibly student leaders, though their plates are often full).

The central management of a mentoring program is essential to coordinating efforts, providing training and support, and ensuring that the program is effective and lasting. Mentoring programs often end up like book clubs – they seem like wonderful ideas that will sustain themselves, but eventually fade due to a lack of intervention and direction. By establishing guidelines, benchmarks, and thorough training, then monitoring the usage and effectiveness of the program, there is a greater guarantee of success. Schools can extend this concept by providing funding and undertaking a full-scale study of their mentoring program. This will generate useful, and hopefully encouraging data.

Level one of the recommended mentoring program is **peer mentoring**. African American freshmen should be matched with juniors or seniors based on intended academic and extracurricular interests. Ideally, these types of mentoring relationships will happen informally, but by formalizing them within a broader retention program, there is now the opportunity to establish benchmarks, training, and assessment.

The central management group should collaborate with the various African American student organizations on campus to identify mentors. This creates partnerships and common objectives, and alleviates potential redundancy, as some organizations may have their own mentoring or buddy systems. After mentors have been selected, they should undergo ample training on topics such as connecting with their mentee, understanding university resources, identifying problems, using effective communications skills, etc.

The interaction between mentors and mentees can vary. At a minimum, mentors should meet face-to-face with their mentees twice a semester and casually assess their social and academic adjustment (based on a recommended list of discussion items provided by the mentor program facilitators). Additionally, mentor/mentee activities can be designated, such as a bowling trip, school football game, or a panel discussion. Students can also connect via e-mail, or mentoring programs can consider setting up an internet discussion board specifically for mentors and mentees to post questions and answers. Some mentor/mentee relationships may not evolve past the minimum standards but others can develop into daily contact, study partners, protégés, and lasting friendships.

Mentors and mentees should do a quantitative review of the program at least twice a year. A small pool should also do a qualitative assessment at least once a year. The central management group should analyze the aggregate results and make the appropriate adjustments to the overall program.

The second mentoring level is **faculty/staff mentoring**. This arrangement could be a one-on-one connection, or through Faculty/Staff/Student interactions (workshops, mixers, panel discussions, presentations, etc). These events provide informal opportunities for students and staff/faculty to develop mutual bonds based on interests and personalities. Faculty and staff should be provided with training, which could be as informal as a group discussion on expectations and objectives of the program. They should also be given a checklist of items to monitor and should engage their student mentees at least once a month – e-mail check-ins, lunch, office hours, etc. Again, both the mentor and mentee should formally assess the program.

The third level of mentoring is **alumni mentoring**. This can be easily facilitated by exchanging student and alumni e-mail addresses based on academic areas of interest. Alumni training will be more difficult, but the central management group can e-mail alums periodic updates and tips for maintaining their mentoring relationship, as well as a checklist of objectives and points to cover. In addition to the e-mail relationship, time should be set aside for alums to meet their mentees at homecoming events and other alumni gatherings on campus. This type of connection not only gives students a preview of life after college, but may help keep alums more involved after they leave campus.

Mentoring is not an exact science, and some mentoring relationships will work better than others. By establishing a multi-layered system, students have an opportunity to make connections from different perspectives, and the overall system has a greater chance of success. Students may feel overwhelmed by receiving three mentors at once, so it is recommended that the peer mentor be the first one assigned, over the summer prior to freshman year if possible. The faculty/staff match can happen early in first semester. Alumni mentoring can begin in the spring semester of freshman year or early in the sophomore year. In the best case, some of these relationships will last a lifetime.

Real world connections

In order for students to fully appreciate the bigger picture, they need to understand how their education translates to their future aspirations. This can occur through mentoring relationships (alumni, staff/faculty), presentations and workshops, and in the home. Parents and extended family members can offer numerous career examples and heart-to-hearts to provide direction and encouragement.

Instill purpose, pride, and responsibility

Taking a page from the traditional segregated single-room schoolhouses, we need to again encourage our students to be the best and to overcome any obstacles. Students must be made to understand that it's not simply about individual success, but that their efforts represent the strength and abilities of our people. We all need an occasional reminder of the advantages we have before us, and the work that needs to be done. Getting this message at home and at school will help keep students focused and committed to the task at hand. Be affirming in your approach, but at times, a stern "talking to" may be necessary as well.

Set expectations

Similar to the above suggestion, imagine how a student will respond in a course in which the professor has personally recognized their work and encouraged them to continue the good performance. Or a professor may tell an average-performing student, "speak up more in class because I know you have something to say," or "you've been doing well, but I believe that you can do even better."

When teachers discount a student from the start, or fail to encourage them, little is done to enhance a student's potential performance. Setting high expectations motivates students to raise their own standards. Let students know what you expect of them, then hold them to it.

Regular check-ins

Parents and family members may feel awkward about initially reaching out to their "baby" once they've gone off to school. You want to give them their space, but you'll also be anxious to hear how they're adjusting. Let them make the first call home, then set up a regular time to touch base. For me and my folks, it was Sunday evenings. With cell phone technology and e-mail now, I know of students who maintain closer ties with their family and speak almost daily. Go with whatever is comfortable for you and your child.

Meet them half way

Parents, mentors, faculty, etc. – know that once a student begins college, they're going through a whirlwind of changes. They may not feel comfortable in their new environment, or may not know how to apply all of the steps listed in this book, especially those that involve connecting with other people (approaching a professor, going to office hours). If you see a question lingering in their head, consider making the first step to draw it out. Create opportunities to engage students and then allow them to open up.

Summary: Develop communities

Students benefit from seeing college as more than a place of stress and academics. If they feel a connection to the people around them, and if they feel supported back home, they'll be encouraged to push themselves. The more positives we can generate, the better. Students are going to struggle, and sometimes knowing that they have someone to lean on – and to push them when necessary – will be what gets them through.

CONCLUSION

A lengthy passage rehashing all of the details that we've covered in this book is not necessary. Hopefully you've read through the information and have absorbed it, personalizing it to meet your needs. As you progress in your college career, use this book to remind you of your purpose, the goals you've set, and the road that you must travel to reach them.

If my words have touched something in your soul and can motivate you to truly challenge yourself, then I have done my job. So many people have sacrificed so much throughout our history so that we can have the opportunities before us today. We owe them more than we can ever pay. It is up to us to learn their stories and continue their work. We will be the ones to pave the paths to tomorrow. Seize the moment, recognize your responsibilities, and never take this opportunity for granted.

Do it for the teachers who inspired you, the family and friends who encouraged you, and the parents who nurtured you. Do it to continue the rich legacy of our people. Do it because there is yet so much that still needs to be done. But most of all, do it for yourself. You are the example of excellence that others shall follow. Believe it, then be it.

Acknowledgements

I always end up doing my acknowledgements at the last minute and fear that I'll forget someone, so if I do, I apologize.

There are many people who made this project possible, directly and indirectly: My parents, for their guidance and for giving me the freedom to follow my heart. My family for their support and love. W.E.B. Du Bois College House (Dr. Stevenson, Sonia Elliott, former GAs and students), for the memories and for allowing me to be a part of the vision. Dr. Marina Barnett-King and Dr. Karl Janowitz, for believing so much in my abilities. The Ase Board, staff, and students, for being a guiding example of what an idea can become. My co-workers (Jean Luc, Lamont, and Kyle), for sticking with it until the end and having my back. Bucktown and the Du Bois Bowl collective, for defying the odds and making things happen. Old college friends, roommates, professors, and mentors, for the experiences and wisdom. I was thinking of many of you as I wrote these pages.

Extra appreciation goes to Juana Gatson for the research, feedback, and edits (you kept me on schedule!), Joy Dyer for the ideas, energy, research, and hustling, and Darnel Degand for the last minute layout consultation.

Notes

Introduction
1. The Education Trust, "Empty Caps and Gowns."
2. The Census Bureau, "Black Population in the United States: March 2002."
3. Federal Bureau of Prisons, "Quick Facts."
4. "Why Aren't There More Blacks Graduating From College?" *The Journal of Blacks in Higher Education*, No. 30 (Winter, 2000-2001), p. 90.
5. Ibid, p. 91.

Chapter Three
1. B. D. Tatum, *Why Are All the Black Kids Sitting Together in the Cafeteria* (New York: Basic Books, 1997) p. 24.
2. L.B. Gallien, Jr. and M. S. Peterson, *Instructing and Mentoring the African American College Student* (New York: Pearson Education, Inc., 2005), p. 124.
3. Ibid, p. 7.
4. T. Perry, C. Steele, and A. Hilliard. *Young, Gifted, and Black: Promoting High Achievement Among African-American Students.* (Boston: Beacon Press, 2003), p. 120.
5. An example is the famous Clark study, discussed in this article: American Psychological Association. "Segregation Ruled Unequal, and Therefore Unconstitutional."

Chapter Four
1. L.B. Gallien, Jr. and M. S. Peterson, *Instructing and Mentoring the African American College Student*, p. 108.
2. C. Johnson and D. Johnson, Learning Power, p. xi.

Chapter Six
1. B. D. Tatum, *Why Are All the Black Kids Sitting Together in the Cafeteria,* p. 62.

Chapter Seven
1. L.B. Gallien, Jr. and M. S. Peterson, *Instructing and Mentoring the African American College Student*, p. 127.
2. Ibid, 130-133.
3. Ibid, 136-138.

Chapter Eight
1. Merriam-Webster Dictionary, Online edition.

Chapter Sixteen

1. Center for Disease Control and Prevention, "Black or African American Populations"
2. Ibid.
3. National Center for Health Statistics. "Prevalence of Overweight and Obesity in Adults in the United States."
4. M. Chiffriller, "Drink Water for Your Health."
5. National Sleep Foundation, "Top Ten Sleep Tips."

Chapter Seventeen

1. MyStudentBody.com, "Interactive STD Prevention Targeting College Students."
2. National Institute of Allergy and Infectious Diseases. "HIV/AIDS Statistics."
3. Center for Disease Control and Prevention, "Black or African American Populations."
4. D. Walhberg, "HIV Study is Chilling to Black College Campuses."
5. The Alan Guttmacher Institute. "An Overview of Abortion in the United States."
6. Rape Treatment Center, UCLA Medical Center. "Rape Facts."
7. University of Illinois Counseling Center. "A Guide for Friends, Family, and Partners: How to Help the Survivor."
8. Ibid.
9. Rape Treatment Center, UCLA Medical Center. "Campus Rape."

Chapter Nineteen

1. P. Vogt, "Five Signs You Should Change Your Major."

Chapter Twenty-Two

1. W.E.B. Du Bois, *Dusk of Dawn* Millwood, New York: Kraus Thomson, 1989. p. 199-200.

Bibliography

Africana.com. "Health Watch: A Healthy Diet." [cited 17 June 2004].
Available from
http://www.africana.com/columns/carson/bl_health_11.asp.

The Alan Guttmacher Institute. "An Overview of Abortion in the United
States." [updated January 2003; cited 17 June 2004]. Available
from http://www.guttmacher.org/presentations/abort_slides.pdf.

Ahmad, Shaheena. *The Yale Daily News Guide to Succeeding in
College*. New York: Kaplan Books, 1997.

American Psychological Association. "Segregation Ruled Unequal, and
Therefore Unconstitutional. [cited 5 June 2004]. Available from
http://www.psychologymatters.org/clark.html.

Anthony, William and Camille Anthony. *The Art of Napping at Work:
The No-Cost, Natural Way to Increase Productivity and
Satisfaction.* Burdett, NY: Larson Publications, 1999.

Armstrong, Thomas. "Multiple Intelligences." [cited 10 June 2004].
Available from
http://www.thomasarmstrong.com/multiple_intelligences.htm.

The Census Bureau. "The Black Population in the United States:
March 2002." [updated April 2003; cited 16 July 2004]. Available
from http://www.census.gov/prod/2003pubs/p20-541.pdf.

Center for Disease Control and Prevention. "Black or African American
Populations." [updated 9 June 2004; cited 17 June 2004].
Available from http://www.cdc.gov/omh/Populations/BAA/BAA.htm.

Center for Disease Control and Prevention. "CDC Statement on
Results of Diabetes Prevention Program." [updated 17 January
2003; cited 17 June 2004]. Available from
http://www.cdc.gov/diabetes/news/docs/dpp.htm.

Center for Disease Control and Prevention. "Eliminate Disparities
in Cardiovascular Disease (CVD)." [updated 9 June 2004; cited 17
June 2004]. Available from
http://www.cdc.gov/omh/AMH/factsheets/cardio.htm.

Chiffriller, Margaret. "Drink Water for Your Health." [cited 17 June 2004]. Available from http://breastcancer.about.com/library/weekly/aa020603a.htm.

Cornel Center for Learning and Teaching. "Study Skills Resources." [cited 10 June 2004]. Available from http://www.clt.cornell.edu/campus/learn/SSWorkshops/ SKResources.html.

Dartmouth Academic Skills Center. "Learning Strategies: Maximizing Your Academic Experience." [updated 12 April 2004; cited 10 June 2004]. Available from http://www.dartmouth.edu/~acskills/ success/index.html.

Dickinson, Dee. "Learning Through Many Kinds of Intelligence." From New Horizons for Learning [internet resource]. [cited 10 June 2004]. Available from http://www.newhorizons.org/strategies/mi/dickinson_mi.html.

Du Bois, W.E.B. *Dusk of Dawn*. Millwood, NY: Kraus Thomson, 1989.

Duke University Academic Resource Center. "Academic Skills Instructional Program." [cited 10 June 2004]. Available from http://aaswebsv.aas.duke.edu/skills/ASIPwebsite/asiphome.html.

The Education Trust. "Empty Caps and Gowns." [updated 26 May 2004; cited 16 July 2004]. Available from http://www2.edtrust.org/EdTrust/Press+Room/ higher+ed+report.htm.

Federal Bureau of Prisons. "Quick Facts." [updated May 2004; cited 16 July 2004]. Available from http://www.bop.gov/fact0598.html.

Felder, Richard M. "Matters of Style." In *ASEE Prism,* 6(4), 18-23. [via internet]. [cited 10 June 2004]. Available from http://www.ncsu.edu/felder-public/Papers/LS-Prism.htm.

Frank, Steven. *The Everything Study Book*. Holbrook, MA: Adams Media Corp., 1996.

Gallien, Louis B., and Marshalita Sims Peterson. *Instructing and Mentoring the African American College Student: Strategies for Success in Higher Education.* New York: Pearson Education, Inc., 2005.